TONG,

ON A SUMMER'S DAY;

THE FORBIDDEN UNION;

AND OTHER POEMS.

BY

ROBERT CARRICK WILDON.

PRINTED FOR THE AUTHOR.

LEEDS:

CHRISTOPHER KEMPLAY, PRINTER, 19, COMMERCIAL-STREET.

1850.

THE FOLLOWING POEMS

ARE

DEDICATED,

WITH THE MOST PROFOUND RESPECT,

TO COLONEL TEMPEST,

OF TONG HALL,

DEPUTY LIEUTENANT OF YORKSHIRE,

BY

THE AUTHOR.

To the Reader.

Whatever little poetic talent the Author may possess, he must honestly confess that he is altogether unacquainted with the art of preface writing; for " rude is he in speech, and little would he grace his cause in speaking for himself;" therefore he must cut as short as possible his introductory speech to the following pages.

It is a common practice with writers of his class to offer a thousand excuses for having ventured to lay their works beneath the eye of a discriminating public ; but the Author of the present volume has no excuse to offer, no apology to make, no friends to accuse of having induced him to take this step; for, although he might say with truth that several literary friends advised him to try a publication, yet he can assure the reader that

the advice of friends could not have led him to
enter on such an undertaking, had he not been
himself desirous to do so,—an undertaking which he
commenced with a despairing heart. But he is
now proud to acknowledge, with the deepest feelings
of gratitude, that his success has already been
greater than his humble hopes at first anticipated;
and he begs to return his most sincere thanks to
the Nobility, Gentry, and Public at large, who
have kindly tendered him the honor of their sup-
port, more especially to his truly generous Patron,
Colonel TEMPEST, to whom, as well as to the
other members of that gentleman's family, he
never can be sufficiently thankful for the great
kindness they have manifested towards one of the
humblest of the sons of song. The author is
only sorry that his feeble efforts are not more
worthy of such high favour; he, however, sin-
cerely hopes they will at least reflect no discredit
either upon himself or his distinguished Patrons.

To the critics he has only to say that he is an
uneducated man, never having been at any school

except one of the commonest kind, held by a
Mr. W. Moore, in the upper part of a cottage in
Bradford, the Author's native town; and the
greatest portion of his Poems have been composed
during his hours of toil, and penned down at night
for pastime and amusement: he is, therefore, well
aware that works produced under such circum-
stances cannot be without faults and blemishes.
Notwithstanding this, he has no favour to ask at the
hands of the critics more than a fair and impartial
consideration of his opportunities for the pursuit of
literary attainments. It will be sufficient satisfaction
to the Author's mind if they " Nothing extenuate,
nor set down aught in malice."

With these brief remarks he launches his little
bark—to sink or swim—upon the broad sea of
public opinion, amidst whose turbulent waves it
must, at all hazards, prove its future destiny.

THE AUTHOR.

SUBSCRIBERS' NAMES.

		COPIES.
Rt. Hon. the EARL OF CARLISLE, K.G. Duchy of Lancaster Office	.	2
Rt. Hon. EARL FITZWILLIAM . Milton	.	1
Rt. Hon. LORD WHARNCLIFFE . Wortley . . .	.	1
Rt. Hon. Viscountess MOUNTGARRETT Nidd Hall . . .	.	1
Colonel TEMPEST, J.P. . . Tong Hall . . .	.	10
Mrs. TEMPEST . . . . Do. . . .	.	4
Miss SARAH TEMPEST . . . Do. . . .	.	2
Miss F. M. R. CURRER . . Eshton Hall . . .	.	1
Mrs. LAMPLUGH W. WICKHAM . Low Moor House . .	.	1
Rev. JOHN BURNET, L.L.D. . . Vicarage, Bradford .	.	2
Rev. WIILIAM DIXON, M.A. . . Tong	.	2
H. W. WICKHAM, Esq., J.P. . . Kirklees Hall . .	.	2
TITUS SALT, Esq., J.P. . . Crow Nest . . .	.	2
JOSHUA POLLARD, Esq., J.P. . Scarr Hall . . .	.	1
W. WALKER, Esq., J.P. . . Bolling Hall . .	.	2
H. A. HARRIS, Esq., J.P. . . Spring Lodge . .	.	1
W. FIELD, Esq. . . . Dudley Hill . .	.	10
SAMUEL LAYCOCK, Esq., J.P. . Bradford . . .	.	2
CHARLES HARDY, Esq., J.P. . Odsal House . .	.	1
T. G. CLAYTON, Esq., J.P. . Bierley Hall . .	.	1

COPIES.

William Rand, Esq., J.P.	Bradford	1
Samuel Smith, Esq., J.P.	Field House	1
Sir Charles R. Tempest, Bart.	Broughton Hall	1
Sir Thomas Beckett, Bart.	Somerley Park	1
William Beckett, Esq., M.P.	Kirkstall Grange	1
M. T. Baines, Esq., M.P.	Somerset House, London	1
E. Denison, Esq., M.P.	Doncaster	1
Henry Edwards, Esq., M.P.	Hope Hall	1
W. R. C. Stansfield, Esq., M.P.	Esholt Hall	1
F. H. Fawkes, Esq., J.P.	Farnley Hall	1
Colonel Pollard, J.P.	Stannary Hall	1
Edward Akroyd, Esq., J.P.	Denton Park	1
J. Milnes Stansfeld, Esq.	Manor House, Flockton	1
Henry Forbes, Esq., J.P., Mayor	Bradford	1
Robert Milligan, Esq., J.P.	Acacia House	1
W. Bower, Esq.	Adwalton	1
Joseph Hargreaves, Esq.	Westgate Hill, near Bradford	1
Thos. Oddy, Esq.	Do. Do.	1
Mrs. Gott	Armley House	2
J. S. Stanhope, Esq.	Cannon Hall	1
Henry Harris, Esq.	Heaton Hall	2
J. Rhodes. Esq.	Adwalton	1
William Wordsworth, Esq.	Blackgates, near Leeds	1
John Hardy, Esq.,	3, Portland Place, London	1
T. L. P. Cunliffe, Esq.	Addingham	1
J. W. T. Vernon Wentworth, Esq.	Wentworth Castle	1
W. Busfeild, Esq., M.P.	Upwood	1
Gathorne Hardy, Esq.	35, Eaton Square, London	1
Radford Potts, Esq.	Beverley	1
Rev. J. Barber, M.A.	Bierley	1

		COPIES.
J. FIELD, Esq.	Stanningley	1
J. RHODES, Esq.	Adwalton	1
J. HAIGH, Esq.	Do.	1
R. WAINHOUSE, Esq., J.P.	Halifax	1
Miss FIELD	Worsbro', Barnsley	1
J. BAXENDALE, Esq.	Bradford	1
D. HANNAM, Esq.	Bowling Lane	1
GEORGE ACKROYDE, Esq.,	Bradford	1
T. NALTON, Esq.	Cheapside, Bradford	2
T. GILLHAM, Esq.	Kirkgate, Bradford	1
Mr. JOHN SHIRES	Holme Lane	1
Mr. A. HAINSWORTH	Do.	1
Mr. A. HOPKINSON	Do.	1
Mr. JOSEPH HOPKINSON	Do.	1
Mr. D. HOPKINSON	Do.	1
Mr. JOHN HOPKINSON	Do.	1
Mr. B. GUMMERSALL	Do.	1
Mr. MEYNELL, Innkeeper	Bowling	1
Mr. J. CLARK	Do.	1
Mr. W. HOPKIN	Tong Street	1
Mr. G. WEBSTER	Adwalton	1
Mr. J. STEAD	Dudley Hill	1
Mr. J. HARROWBY	Horton Lane, Bradford	1
Mr. J. REDMAYNE	Tong	1
Mr. W. DAY	Tong Street	1
Mr. A. ELSWORTH	Do.	1
Mr. B. ELLIS	Dudley Hill	1
Mr. J. FARRER	Do.	1
Mr. J. A. WILDON	Ashton-under-Lyne	1
Mr. N. SCHOEFIELD	Do.	1

xii.

COPIES.

Miss Haughton	Ashton-under-Lyne	1
Mr. J. Robson	Wakefield Road, Bradford	3
Mr. E. Haley	Bowling	1
Mr. J. Gummersall	Tong Street	1
Mr. S. Hargreaves	Do.	1
Mr. J. Rhodes	Bedlam Farm	1
Mr. H. Midgley	Tong Street	1
Mr. J. Thomes	Do.	1
Mr. David Sutcliffe	Dudley Hill	1
Mr. F. Kendal	Wakefield Road	1
Mr. John Rayner	Green House, Pudsey	1
Mr. John Ellis	Dudley Hill	1
Mr. J. Ellis	Leeds Road, Bradford	1
Mr. Denis Ellis	Dudley Hill	1
Mr. White	Halifax	1
Mr. Michael Schofield	Sticker Lane, Bowling	12
Mr. A. Marsden	Cutler Heights, Bowling	1
Mr. Thos. Firth	Tong Street	1
Mr. Nathan Fisher	Do..	1
Mr. V. Dobson	Do.	1
Miss Sarah Ann Greenhough	Birkenshaw	1
Mr. Brook Lister	Do.	1
Mr. E. Lister	Do.	1
Mr. G. Bond	Holme Lane	1
Mr. J. Sharp	Brighouse	1
Mr. J. Phillips	Tong Street	1
Mr. J. Booth	Dudley Hill	1
Mr. S. Auty	Manchester Road, Bradford	1
E. Clapham, Esq.	Manningham	1
J. Johnson, Esq.	Ashton-under-Lyne	1

			COPIES.
Mr. JONAS WILKINSON	Bowling		1
Mr. ROBERT HOLMES	Tong Street		1
Mr. EDWARD TETLEY	Ditto		1
Mr. THOMAS WOOD	Ashton-under-Lyne		1
Mr. H. WILDON	Ditto		1
Mr. W. PRIESTLEY	Dudley Hill		1
Mr. T. R. CHARLESWORTH	Bowling		1
Mr. FIRTH DENISON	Mountserrat House		1
Mr. SAMUEL LODGE, Surgeon	Dudley Hill		2
Mr. J. CLOUGH	Halifax		1
Mr. W. MUFF	Dudley Hill		1
Mr. M. HESELTINE	Bowling		1
Mr. W. BARNES	Ditto		1
Mr. J. RAPIER	Dudley Hill		1
Mr. J. HUNT	New Halifax		2
Mr. W. HAINSWORTH	Dudley Hill		1
Mr. THOS. WILDON	Macclesfield		1
Mr. E. HAIGH	Bradford		1
Miss S. MARGARETTS	Bourton-on-the-Hill, Gloucester		1
Miss LAMB	Tong		1
Mrs. B. GUMMERSALL	Tyresall Hall		1
Mr. J. BUCKLEY	Ashton-under-Lyne		1
Mr. J. COOK	Vicar Lane, Bradford		2
Mr. J. SWAIN	Horton Lane, Bradford		1
Mr. J. TILL	Vicar Lane, Leeds		1
Mr. J. ODDY	Tong Street		1
Mr. J. BARRACLOUGH	Adwalton		1
Mr. W. BARRACLOUGH	Do.		1
Mr. M. TROUGHTON	Do.		1
Mr. J. HUDSON	Tong Street		1

		COPIES.
Mr. E. Swithinbank . .	Bradford . . .	. 1
Mr. J. Pitts . . .	Tong Street . . .	. 1
Mr. W. Sykes . . .	Bradford . . .	. 1
Mr. J. Tetley . .	Do.	. 1
Mr. W. Handby . .	Do.	. 1
Mr. W. Rooks . .	Do.	. 1
Mr. J. Rowley . .	Do.	. 1
Mr. W. O. Walls . .	Do.	. 1
Mr. W. Lambert . .	Do.	. 1
Mr. W. Taylor . .	Do.	. 1
Mr. William Walls .	Do.	. 1
Mr. Samuel Cooper .	Idle	. 1
Mr. Joel West . .	Dudley Hill . .	. 1
Mr. E. Carr . . .	Dudley Hill . .	. 1 .
Mrs. Scholfield . .	Do.	. 1
Mrs. Garforth . .	Bradford . . .	. 1
Mrs. Mowbray . .	York . . .	. 1
Mr. W. Illingworth .	Do. . . .	. 1
Mr. J. Lucas . . .	Bowling . . .	. 1
Mr. W. Hullah . .	Tong . . .	. 1
Mr. J. Brearcliffe .	Toftshaw . .	. 1
Mr. J. Berry . .	Do. . . .	. 1

MANY SUBSCRIBERS' NAMES ARRIVED TOO LATE FOR INSERTION.

CONTENTS.

TONG,

ON A SUMMER'S DAY.

Half screened by its trees in the sabbath's calm smile,
  The Church of our forefathers, how meekly it stands !
O villagers, gaze on its old hallowed pile,
  It was dear to their hearts, it was raised by their hands.
Who loves not the spot where they worshipped their God ?
  Who loves not the spot where their ashes repose ?
Dear even the daisy that blooms on the sod,
  For dear is the dust out of which it arose.

Then say, shall the Church which our forefathers built,
  Which the tempests of ages have battled in vain ;
Abandoned by us from supineness or guilt,—
  O say, shall it fall by the rash, the profane ?
No, perish the impious hand that would take
  One shred from its altars, one stone from its towers ;
The life's blood of martyrs was shed for its sake,
  And its fall—if it fall—shall be reddened with ours.

ROBERT STORY.

Enchanting view ! how beautiful thou art,
What boundless joy thy prospects can impart !
From busy town the poet might retire,
In this sweet place to tune his simple lyre ;
To roam through woods, or sit by gurgling stream,
Soaring to heaven as in a waking dream ;

All earthly troubles for the time forgot,
Wrapped in the charms of this delightful spot.
All that is heard and all the eye may see
Seem framed for love and peace and poesy;
The fields enamelled with a thousand dyes,
Where the soft violet with the primrose vies;
The king-cup bending in its golden pride,
While sheets of daisies smile on every side;
The pale wild rose on verdant hedges seen,
And woodbine sweet perfumes the bower of green,
In whose cool shade the linnet swells his throat,
And rapture flows on every gentle note;
While all around the sky-larks swiftly rise,
And warbling softly flutter to the skies;
The blackbird whistles loudly in the glade,
The mellow thrush lends all his power to aid;
The goldfinch yields his unassuming lay,
The blackcap carols on the bending spray;
The gentle redbreast tunes his little song,
Striving his best to help the happy throng;
And hosts are busy of the feathery tribes
Of kinds more various than my pen describes;
Some gathering moss their artful nests to form,
Or softest down to line and make them warm;
While others haste from place to place along,
Seeking provisions for their helpless young.

The full-blown woods in richest foliage clad
Wave in the air and make the landscape glad;
Beneath whose boughs the wild and swift-winged doves
Sidle and coo, and tell their happy loves;

The pheasants rise on wings all bright and gay,
Spreading their plumage in the sunny ray ;
The timid hare bounds o'er the level plain,
Now stopping short, now darting on again ;
The little bees through woods and meadows haste,
Alighting oft each blooming bud to taste,
Collecting treasures all the live-long hours,
Extracting sweets from many poisonous flowers ;
From tree to tree, from bush to bush, they roam,
And bear their loads on silken pinions home,
There store it up within each waxen cell,
Where through the winter 'tis their hope to dwell ;
Thus when loud Boreas brings his frost and storm,
Their sombre homes are filled with food, and warm ;
Myriads of insects wisk and hum around
Filling the air with many a mingling sound.
All nature seems in animation now,
Active with life around, above, below :—
The sturdy mower plies his glittering scythe,
While others follow diligent and blithe,
Spreading the grass beneath the summer's heat,
Which loads the air with odours softly sweet ;
The rustic peasants whistle at their teams,
Inured to storms, and to the scorching beams ;
The useful farmer with unwearying hand
Toils through the day among the fertile land,
And smiles with joy to see the ripening grain,
To find his labour has not been in vain.
Here are the cattle in the pasture green,
And harmless flocks are in the distance seen,
Ten thousand charms in nature's lap here lie,

To glad the ear, and to delight the eye;
In each fair scene, in each harmonious sound,
The source, the soul of poesy is found.
O ! while so many fret away their life
In party quarrel and in wordy strife,
Let me roam forth amid these rural views,
In sweet communion with the humble muse ;
Straying by many a softly singing brook,
Indulging long in nature's mighty book,
In every page of which great work I find
Something wherewith to elevate the mind;
From every bud, from every leaf that grows,
A boundless store of useful knowledge flows ;
From each small herb that in the meadow springs,
From each sweet bird that in the woodland rings ;
Each little berry on the hedges borne,
Each blade of grass, each separate ear of corn,
All the bright things that decorate the field,
Instruction sound to thankless man may yield ;
The slender sprig, the grain, the towering tree,
Confess the presence of a Deity.—
O, where is he who on this path has trod,
And still denies the being of a God ?
Impious wretch, behold yon clear blue sky,
See yon broad orb in all his pomp on high,
Observe the waters rolling on the way,
The toilsome bee, the butterfly so gay ;
Mark the fair copse, the hills, the sloping dales,
Their pages read, and learn their truthful tales ;
Talk to the bush, the bloom, the scented bower,
Speak to them all,—they own a Supreme Power,

All nature seems with one according voice
To bless His might, and in His love rejoice.

Further I roam along this valley green,
The more I love each freshly rising scene;
The brooklet's course with pleasure I pursue,
Its rippling stream in varying shapes to view,
Here winding onward through a thorny maze,
Now sparkling clearly where the bright trout plays;
Here rolls it softly o'er its sandy bed
And there it forms a little wild cascade;
Then through the wood it murmurs on its way
Where spreading boughs exclude the light of day;
And there its waters such sweet sounds impart
As kindle rapture in the poet's heart;
No famous minstrel could delight his ear
With such a harp as swells—unceasing—here.
Oft here the poacher's ringing shot is heard,
And to the earth down drops the quivering bird;
Full often here is spread the fatal snare,
To trap and slay the unsuspecting hare;
While o'er the fields his dogs in silence speed,
As though they knew 'twere an unlawful deed.

Still with the streamlet let me roam along
Through Scholbrook vale, and by the park of Tong;
'Tis true I trespass on the farmer's fields,
The danger risking for the joy it yields;
But let not Hopkin murmur at the crime,
'Tis but to seek materials for my rhyme;
No fence I'd break, nor mar his yellow grain,

Nor hedge, nor wall, shall injury sustain ;
I trespass merely to enjoy alone
All nature's children full and fairly blown.

O, for a cell these sylvan scenes among!
My home the woods, my friends the warbling throng,
Their notes by day my solitude to fill,
By night the music of the tinkling rill ;
In this sequestered, lonesome spot to dwell,
Hemmed in by brake, by dingle, and by dell,
'Twere all I'd wish, 'twere all I could desire,
Here would I live, and here at last expire;
Here spend my summers like a happy bird,
Where naught of man's tumultuous broils are heard;
Leaving my couch o'er hill and dale to stray,
Gazing on nature in her best array ;
To view bright flowerets rising in each glade
To watch them bloom, and sigh to see them fade.
Little I'd ask wherewith to bless my cave,
No silken robes, no riches would I crave ;
Humble and cleanly take my simple food,
And for that morsel shed no creature's blood ;
For my support no pheasant e'er should die,
No gentle dove upon my platters lie ;
No partridge fair should pant in death for me,
No sportive rabbit my repast should be ;
No tender leveret should its life resign
To be the means of still preserving mine.
No, those fair things I would with care defend,
And have them know me only as their friend ;
My board should be with simplest food supplied,

With no display of luxury or pride.
O blissful thought ! to spend the happy hours
'Mid flowery groves, sweet birds, and fragrant bowers ;
Where ample floods of inspiration spring
From all around, from every little thing.

Then, as stern Autumn might be creeping round,
When trees cast off their clothing to the ground,
When hills and dales look desolate and bare,
And cold sleet floating on the frosty air;
Straight to my rocky dwelling I'd retire
And make me up a little cheering fire,
Partake my meal with all a hermit's pride,
And thank my God for that He might provide ;
There pass the moments like a lone recluse,
There still untiring woo the bashful muse ;
There sit and hear the swelling of the flood
Moan o'er its bed or roar along the wood.
And if some chance at eventide should bring
The lonesome robin near my cave to sing,
How would I strive to coax the wanderer in,
And use much care his confidence to win ;
With gentle hand his form should be caressed,
I'd give him food, and warm him in my breast ;
Bid him no more in plaintive cadence mourn,
But sing with hope of cheering Spring's return ;
Then should his song make glad my woodland cave,
While winds without might roar, and swell and rave ;
How sweetly thus the wintry months would fly
With none to mar my solitude and joy.— *
My dream is passed, the blissful vision flown,

Delusive fancy drops the curtain down ;
And I, alas, perceive that dream to be
Too bright to be e'er realized for me.

Onward I stroll along the park-wall side
And up the hill, with all a poet's pride ;
Here I sit down upon a grassy mound
Gazing with joy on every thing around ;
Here the sweet breath of nature I inhale
From rosy hedges and the verdant vale.
O, how I feel my very soul essay
To leave this sordid tenement of clay ;
To soar unfettered through yon boundless space,
And thank my God for His unceasing grace ;
To bless His name, and yield the praise we owe
For these fair scenes, for all He does bestow.

All slowly now the lofty hill I rise,
And soon the village meets my gladsome eyes ;
Delightful Tong ! that seem'st to know no dearth,
Thou'rt like a Heaven on this poor spot of earth.
He who is weary of the town's turmoil,
And seeks a refuge from its noise and broil,
Let him straightway to this fair village come,
Here build his cot and make a happy home ;
Here might he dwell and feel supremely blest,
With no confusion to disturb his rest ;
No sound is heard save what from labour springs,—
The blacksmith's bellows moan, the anvil rings ;
The lowly cots—so humble and so clean,
Their ancient casements hung with ivy green—

Seem to bespeak the happy homes within,
Unknown to tumult and unknown to sin;
While little gardens flourish here and there,
Whose fragrant breath perfumes the gentle air.
O, 'tis a spot where kings might deign to dwell,
Too fair indeed for my poor muse to tell.

The aged church must next attention draw,
Filling the soul with reverential awe;
Beneath whose roof soft hymns of praise are given,
And fervent prayers devoutly breathed to Heaven.
The much loved pastor often have I seen
(On Sabbath morns) conducting o'er the green
A youthful train, with all a father's care,
From village school to this the house of prayer;
In whose apt minds his pious wish would raise
A love for bliss that knows no end of days.
Here are his counsels faithfully set forth,
And precepts pure of more than golden worth;
Kindly he points them on the righteous way,
Imploring Heaven to guard them day by day;
His sacred doctrines truly can impart
Fresh gleams of hope to the despairing heart;
The aged listen with attentive ears,
And deep contrition melts them into tears.
O where are they this edifice that raised,
And at its altar first their Maker praised?
Where the divines? and where the pastors' grave,
Who their advice to our forefathers gave?
Where are they now? gone hence, alas, where we

Must shortly follow, as they are, to be.
O hallowed pile! on which I musing look,
Thou seem'st to me an ever open book,
Full of stern facts which cannot be denied,
That speak aloud of human pomp and pride.
Its pages tell how vain man's projects are,
Whether in commerce, or in fields of war ;
All end the same, the monarch and the slave,
All, all conclude by coming to the grave ;
The church-yard swallows each succeeding age,
And none escape, nor youth, nor bearded sage.
Man lives to day in health and strength and bloom,
To-morrow comes and takes him to the tomb ;
Grim Death stalks round, and not a favour shows,
But deals to all his never-failing blows ;
The artless child, the laughter-loving maid
On whose fair cheek the glow of beauty played ;
The brawny peasant, and the worn-out hind,
Within this wall one common lodging find ;
Which proves how vain man's hopes, however bright,
Formed in the morn to perish ere 'tis night.
Life, transient life, is like the soft March flower
That springs at noon, and evening's frosty shower
Falls on its charms, and nips its bloom away,
Ere it has scarcely peeped above the clay ;
'Tis like a play where changes intervene,
Now comes a gay and now a painful scene,
Shifting about as circumstances do,
Pleasure by times, but much more frequent woe ;
We find a joy our weary path upon,
Which scarce is felt, ere 'tis for ever gone.

Leaving this scene of silence and of gloom,
Soon to the entrance of the Park I come,
Through whose closed gates I look with joy around,
But must not dare within its walls be found ;
Else with what pride I might my walk pursue
Adown this wide, this cooling avenue,
And through the grounds all cheerfully proceed
To watch the pheasant or the partridge feed ;
Or sit me down beneath a shady tree
And frame my songs, from earthly trouble free ;
Or round the hall to wander o'er and o'er,
And every corner, every nook, explore :—
But no, my lot that bliss to me denies ;
Still must I look with longing, lingering eyes ;
More of this place, and of its Hall I'd know,
Of what it might be centuries ago ;
O, with what joy its history should I read,
From page to page with anxious care proceed ;
Where many a tale may doubtlessly be told
Of lady loves, and trusty knights of old.

Perhaps I tread where Airedale's poet trod,
And thoughtful viewed the wondrous works of God :
Unhappy votary at Thalia's shrine !
Sad was thy life, untimely death was thine,
Tossed in the flood to which thou gav'st such praise,
The favorite theme among thy gentle lays ;
Oft hast thou walked within this lofty wall,
Around the Park, and round the ancient Hall.
Then might thy thoughts revert as mine do now,
To days when men forsook the loom and plough,

And raised the flag, and formed rebellious bands,
Seizing the sword with strong and desperate hands;
When fearful currents of intestine broil
Rolled through the land, and marred the fruitful soil;
When death and carnage stalked abroad the while,
Their baneful influence spreading o'er our isle;
A thousand widows every day were made,
A thousand fathers on the cold earth laid;
A thousand children wept for their return,
And shed vain tears to see their mothers mourn.

Then from this Hall perhaps some belted knight
Came boldly forth cased up in armour bright;
Mounting his steed, and with good sword and shield
Rushing like lightning to the battle field,
Resolved to quell the storm of mortal strife,
Or in its waves to sacrifice his life.—
'Twas then, I ween, the name of Tempest rang
Along the plain, amid war's awful clang;
A host of swords flashed forth at that loved name,
By stout arms drawn, and backed by hearts the same;
True loyal hearts that would have fought and bled,
And onward pressed where'er their lord had led.—
Ah, those dread times brought every kind of scathe,
Want, woe and blood, and pestilence and death.
Though fierce commotions still our nation fill,
Yet midst it all no human blood we spill;
No clash of swords the affrighted ears assail,
No cannons' roar disturb the peaceful vale;
Though wild contentions rage both near and far,
'Tis but the tumult of a paper war.

Ah, no, how changed! sweet Peace with happy smile
Sheds her soft halo o'er our native isle;
The generous Tempest of our own calm age
Seeks not for fame amid the battle's rage;
No barbed charger bears him o'er the plain,
Amongst the heaps of wounded and of slain;
'Tis his to cheer the lonesome widow's state,
'Tis his to sooth the hapless orphan's fate;
'Tis his the poor man's sufferings to assuage,
And kindly prop the tottering step of age.
Fair is the fame such worthy deeds award,
Fair the renown that springs from deep regard
Of those who dwell upon his fertile lands,
And feel the favours showered from his hands.
Such is the fame that proves a noble mind,
Such is the fame the truly great would find;
Such the renown, and such the lasting praise
That crowns the Tempest of our own good days.
Let none exclaim, and say the poet plays
A flatterer's part, though humble be his lays,—
No much he'd scorn from honest truth to swerve,
To praise the man his praise might not deserve;
No knave is he, no mercenary views
Prompt the outpourings of his rustic muse;
Himself has shared —and no contemptuous part—
The open bounty of a Tempest's heart;
And O, may Heaven still his years prolong
To reign beloved o'er these fair grounds of Tong!

But evening comes, and day's resplendent eye
Rolls its bright lustre toward the western sky,

Shedding a light most glorious to behold,
Like one vast sea of purple and of gold.—
O, what soft tints bedeck his fiery crown,
As his rich chariot sinks in splendour down !
Thin summer clouds are gathering fast on high,
The chirping birds to roosting places fly ;
The peacock's scream upon the light breeze floats,
The noisy rooks join their discordant notes ;
The weary mower leaves the meadow now,
While drops of sweat roll off his sunburnt brow ;
The buxom damsel hastens to the field
And calls her kine their evening milk to yield ;
The laden bees wing homeward for the night ;
To coverts thick the wild doves take their flight ;
The busy hum of insects dies away
And seems to perish with departing day ;
The fresh dew falls on every flower and thorn,
Bright spangles forming for another morn ;
The hare now quits the place of her retreat
And with quick eye, and soft and noiseless feet,
To these rich fields of corn or clover speeds,
And here at leisure silently she feeds.
Ah, there she starts to see me passing by
And hastes away with wild reverted eye ;
Poor simple thing, for me no terror feel
The bard would scorn to mar thy joyful meal.
See, now the keepers slowly leave their home,
With arms prepared as o'er the park they roam,
To guard the game 'gainst any poaching throng
Who oft at midnight haunt the grounds of Tong.
While such bold men seek timid hares to slay,

Let me tread homeward on my flowery way ;
And in my cot my simple verses frame,
Tuning the harp unknown to wealth or fame ;
While near me smiles the partner of my life
She who must share my pleasures or my strife ;
And by my knee a little fair haired boy
Looks up and lisps, and yields me matchless joy.
Say not, ye great, the lowly feel no bliss,
When a poor bard declares such joy as this.

Adieu, dear scenes! a little time adieu!
Soon, soon again your woods and vales I'll view ;
Such charms have ye, I cannot leave you long ;
Adieu! sweet spot; adieu! delightful Tong.

THE FORBIDDEN UNION.

A TALE OF THE SEVENTEENTH CENTURY.

CANTO FIRST.

Come forth, my gentle harp, once more,
My dearest wealth, my brightest store;
That store by bounteous nature given,
The life-enduring gift of Heaven.
Come, let me touch thy strings again
And wake—to me—thy pleasing strain;
Though poor to others thou may'st be,
Thou still hast endless charms for me,
Such as can ne'er be bought or sold,
Beyond the price of paltry gold.
Thy notes can soothe my deepest grief,
And yield my drooping heart relief;
When earthly woes my mind beset,
I strike thy chords and all forget.
In thee—whatever ills attend—
I find a constant changeless friend;
Though all the world desert my side,
Thou still art there, my joy, my pride!

Come let us once again inhale
The breath of this inspiring vale,—
The vale of Tong, its fields and woods.
Its bushes, dells, and opening buds;
Whose present state we've sung before:
Now let us try the days of yore,
When civil broil with fiery brand
Destruction spread throughout the land,
When discord swelled with fearful groan
And hurled the monarch from his throne;
When naked swords from scabbards flashed,
And brethren against brethren clashed;
When plumed helms waved in the field,
And many a bright emblazoned shield;
When coats of mail in sun-rays glanced,
And snorting chargers proudly pranced;
When lances glittered on the plain,
And deep-mouthed cannons roared amain;
When banners floated broad and high,
And martial music rent the sky;
When echoes rose from hill and dale
Of orphan's cry or widow's wail.
In those fierce times of strife and storms,
Of battles, sieges and alarms,
There stood in a sequestered spot
Of this sweet vale a snow-white cot,
Which seemed a safe and blest retreat,
Where love and peace might deign to meet.
With roses wild the porch was crowned,
And woodbine gently crept around;
Soft jasmins reared with fondest care

B

Bedecked the cleanly casements there,
And fairest plants of sweet perfume
Grew round it in their lovely bloom.
Its inmates were a happy pair,
Though poor, unknown to rankling care :
Old Conyard's virtuous conduct won
Esteem and love of every one,
And knights and squires would condescend
To call and treat him as a friend ;
And Heaven had blessed him with a wife
Who never caused domestic strife ;
She daily plied her spinning wheel,
And cooked the frugal household meal ;
While Conyard toiled the sunny hours,
By twilight dressed his plants and flowers.
Thus like a seldom ruffled stream,
Or like a long and pleasing dream,
Their lives along Time's channel went,
'Midst gentle peace and sweet content.

And with them dwelt in that calm place
A maiden of unblemished grace ;
With fairy step and sylph-like form,
And many a truly witching charm,
A softly sweet expressive eye
Outshining all the stars on high,
A polished, fair and lofty brow,
As white as is the mountain snow,
While silken curls of auburn hair
Hung graceful o'er her shoulders fair ;
Her lips like rosebuds fresh and new,

Just sprinkled with the morning dew;
Her teeth were tinged with healthy glows,
Like lilies blended with the rose.
O, she was fair as aught on earth,
And rife with innocence and worth;
Ten thousand flowers bloomed sweetly there,
But none with Lucia could compare;
With warbling birds the valley rang
But none like that young maiden sang.
She loved to roam at eventide
Along the murmuring brooklet's side,
To hear the songsters strain their throats,
And join her own melodious notes,
So pure, so thrilling, and so high,
With those sweet beauties of the sky;
Or tune the harp she loved so well,
And wake the echoes of each dell.
Ah, this dear vale would surely then
Have foiled the bard's descriptive pen;
Its tinkling rills, its brakes and glades,
Its sunny walks and cooling shades;
Its darkly frowning moss-crowned rocks,
Fit coverts for the prowling fox;
The gentle lawn, the silent grove,
Where maiden might confess her love;
The sloping hills so fair to view,
All clad with flowers of every hue;
The fruit trees wild shed their perfume,
And waved in air their pleasing bloom;
The aged thorns in white array
Made every hedge surpassing gay.

Still lay the poet's harp unstrung,
And all those charms remained unsung,
Except when Lucia gave it praise
In artless unassuming lays;
Which was but rare, for her young mind
Held subjects of another kind.
She thought of her paternal home,
And groves where she was wont to roam;
Full often wished the wars might end,
And give her back each long-lost friend;
To see her sire's embattled walls,
And tread again his spacious halls:
For she was Earl De Moran's child,
Who oft on her in raptures smiled;
Her mother—when she gave her birth—
Resigned her life and fled from earth,
And Lucia was her father's joy,
A hope, a bliss that ne'er could cloy.
   Thus when rebellion stalked abroad,
And blood and carnage marked its road,
De Moran took his daughter fair,
And placed her 'neath old Conyard's care;
Then leaving that romantic vale,
He donned a shining suit of mail,
And, mounted on his warlike steed,
Dashed over hill and dale with speed,
To where the royal pennons flew,
By heroes guarded firm and true,
Resolved their monarch's rights to shield,
Or bravely die upon the field.
Amongst the numbers gathered there

Of lords and knights from far and near,
None might to greater fame aspire
Than gentle Lucia's noble sire ;
For scarred was he with many a blow
Received in battles long ago ;
And oft he'd borne the prize away
At tournament or mock affray ;
Full many a knight in contest warm
Had felt the prowess of his arm ;
Whenever he assailed his foes,
They reeled beneath his mighty blows.
Although his strength was sinking now,
And age had marked his swarthy brow,
Yet came he there to earn fresh fame
And add more laurels to his name.
He long had won the King's regard,
And now was prompt his rights to guard,
To lend his aid or yield his life
In crushing the intestine strife.
But still the hero's anxious mind
Returned to objects left behind ;
The snow-white cottage of the vale
Would oft his wandering thoughts assail,
And that fair child he held so dear
Did often in his dreams appear.
No foeman braver knight could meet,
No daughter kinder father greet ;
In war his bosom seemed inspired
With lion rage that never tired ;
At home in peace, the playful child
Fearless his gentler mood beguiled.—

Now let us leave the loyal knight
Where ready swords were gleaming bright,
And turn from that heroic throng
Again unto the vale of Tong.

Calm was the eve ; the setting sun
Was closing his diurnal run,
Painting the skies with many a hue,
Bright floods of gold and streaks of blue ;
Soft tinges of his parting beams
A moment played upon the streams,
Then fled to regions of the west,
And all things seemed to sink in rest ;
Then twilight flung its shades around,
And solemn silence reigned profound.
O, 'twas a sweet inspiring hour,
When bard might haunt the grove or bower,
Where nothing could disturb his ear
Save onward waters murm'ring near.
At that loved time a fair youth strayed
Along the vale by heath and glade :
He was—though young—of manly frame,
And strength and vigour might he claim.
With some deep theme his mind seemed fraught,
His brow was marked with pensive thought ;
Slow was his step, and oft he sighed
And touched the rapier at his side.
Proceeding still in serious mood,
He sought the shelter of the wood,
Beneath whose gloomy shades reclined
To musing thought he gave his mind.

He was Sir Rosco's only son,
Who long a brilliant course had run,
Whose breast with martial heat was fired,
By which great fame he had acquired ;
His deeds the monarch's favour gained,
And long had he his place maintained ;
But for some trifling fault at last
He was from all his greatness cast,
And all the lands he then might own
Were confiscated to the crown.
The ire of many an angry vow
Deep marks of pride stamped on his brow ;
And gathering up his private store,
Resolved to serve the king no more,
He left his proud baronial seat,
To seek some distant lone retreat,
Where he amid fair nature's charms
Might train his son to deeds of arms ;
For he had trod the path of fame,
And hoped his boy might do the same.
Ere long their obscure home was made
Near Full-Neck's calm and silent shade ;
But there his name was kept concealed
And rank and fortune unrevealed.
He taught young Rosco day by day
The use of arms in fierce affray :—
And now some rapid years had flown
Since he'd incurred the Sovereign's frown,
And tall and stout his son had grown,
Who longed to join the ranks of war
And seek the bubble fame afar.

The youth oft vowed he'd ne'er return
Till brightest laurels he could earn,
Till proud distinction he could claim
To honor his brave father's name.
On themes like this his thoughts were bent,
As wandering through the vale he went;
And stopping near a moss-clad bank
He mused on titles, wealth and rank;
Vain fancy led him far away
To scenes of grand but stern array,
To fields of blood and sanguine strife,
Of wounds and of departing life;
And his enthusiastic mind
The fearful struggle warmly joined;
In wild, imagination's flight
He rushed into the hottest fight,
And carved his way through thickest foes,
O'erthrowing all that might oppose.
But as he onward, onward pressed,
And thirst of fame inspired his breast,
A voice came floating with the stream,
Destroying that romantic dream;
A voice so sweet past all compare,
Its tones enriched the evening air;
So pure, in sooth, it was, that he
Believed it could not mortal be,
But some kind Angel's from above,
Sent down to sing of peace and love;
And as each soft and tender note
Did on the light-winged zephyrs float,
The roosting birds awoke again,
As thus rung out the stirring strain.

SONG.

Cease, O war, thy dread commotion,
  Stem, O stem, thy fearful flood;
Sheath thy sword o'er land and ocean,
  Longer shed not human blood.
    Let thy cannons roaring loudly,
    Let thy banners waving proudly,
    Lie unused in gentle peace;
    Cease, O war, thy thunders cease!

Quit, O war, thy fierce contentions,
  Desolating this fair land;
Quit thy dark, thy wild dissensions,
  And thy martial troops disband.
    Let thy blood-stained sabres glancing,
    Let thy chargers snorting, prancing,
    Let them rest in happy peace,
    Cease, O war, thy thunders cease!

Many a heart thou wring'st with sadness,
  Fill'st with tears a thousand eyes;
Many a wretch thou driv'st to madness,
  Disuniting warmest ties.
    Spears and lances brightly gleaming
    Over wounds all redly streaming,
    Let those weapons lie in peace,
    Cease, O war, thy thunders cease!

Many a hall and many a bower
  Echo with the widow's moans;
Many a strong embattled tower
  Drowns the pent up prisoner's groans.

O, thy trumpets hoarsely sounding,
Booming drums with tones astounding,
Let them lie in silent peace,
Cease, O war, thy thunders cease !

Longer spread not fear and wonder
  O'er our valleys, hills and plains ;
Stay thy course of scathe and plunder,
  Blood and carnage, death and pains.
    Cot and mansion share thy terrors,
    Lord and peasant feel thy horrors,
    All alike are lost to peace,
    Cease, O war, thy thunders cease !

Warrior turn thee towards thy dwelling,
  Sires your weeping children seek,
Soothe the hearts with sorrow swelling,
  Dry the tear-drop from the cheek.
    Doff, O doff, your fearful armour,
    Leave, O leave, the strife and clamour ;
    Find your homes, reside in peace,
    And let war's dreadful thunders cease !

The cadence died, while brake and cave⎫
Its last long breath in echoes gave,   ⎬
Then all was silent as the grave ;   ⎭
And round and round young Rosco gazed,
Delighted, yet as much amazed ;
When soon a female, fair and light,
Appeared to his astonished sight;
Who from a dingle of the wood

Still nearer came to where he stood;
Not deeming mortal near her then,
She stepped along the lonesome glen ;
Until a stranger spying there,
At once did pause the peerless fair ;
A moment cast her glorious eyes
Upon the youth in deep surprise,
And then, abruptly turning, took
Another pathway to the brook.
He stood transfixed, as one of stone,
And followed with his eyes alone ;
Through gloomy shades of twilight grey
He long could see her light array ;
She crossed the stream with hasty tread,
Along its green embankments sped ;
Reaching the humble cot so white,
She disappeared from Rosco's sight.
Then did the youth bewildered seem
To wake as from a joyful dream,
The voice had died, the form was gone,
And all was silent, drear and lone.
Soft love, with its bewitching smart,
Like magic crept around his heart,
And floods of glory seemed to roll
In blissful raptures through his soul.
Yet doubt and sadness still would find
A place in his unsettled mind ;
And as he left that gay green spot,
Oft turned his eye to yonder cot ;
While many deep unbidden sighs
Would from his struggling bosom rise.

With mingled marks of joy and pain
His home obscure was reached again,
Where soon his couch our hero sought,
And there indulged in deepest thought:
Hope, fear and joy his mind assailed
And through his slumbers still prevailed ;
The maiden form still blessed his sight,
Filling his sleep with warm delight.
Awaking with the morn's first ray,
All sad and unrefreshed he lay,
Scarce knowing what it all might be,
A vision or reality :
That fairy step, that angel form,
That voice with such a wondrous charm,
Had made his youthful bosom swell
With feelings which he could not quell ;
The maid, the cot, the song, the stream,
He strove to count as all a dream ;
And yet meantime the youth would fain
Have dreamed it o'er and o'er again.
Thus passed the morning hours away,
And thus the sultry noontide ray ;
Still, still he struggled to forget
The scenes that had his peace beset.
Yet would intruding hopes take place,
And Fancy brightest pictures trace ;
Then did his heart sincerely yearn
For gentle eventide's return,
That he again might roam along
The sweet enchanting vale of Tong ;
And fondly hoped the lady might

Once more walk forth and bless his sight,
Once more that voice might bliss impart,
And pour bright transports round his heart.

END OF CANTO FIRST.

CANTO SECOND.

Night, blissful night, had calmly drawn
Her curtain over grove and lawn ;
All Nature seemed in deep repose,
No sound from hill or dale arose ;
Each member of the feathery throng
Had chaunted out his evening song ;
The bee had flown from woodlands gay,
Whose humming sound had died away ;
The butterfly had left the flower
To rest in some sweet blossomed bower,
Where her bright wings of varied hue
Were steeped in soft and pearly dew ;
No groan of bending oak was heard,
The trees their foliage scarcely stirred ;
The glowworm 'neath the hawthorn shade
Its little simple light displayed ;
While from above bright rays were given
By all the countless lamps of heaven,
Each flinging forth its twinkling light,
Relieving the dark shades of night;
And 'mid the sparkling host on high
The broad moon rode in majesty,
Reigning like some transcendant Queen
In grandeur o'er the glorious scene.

But who was he at that lone hour,
Who moved by dingle, brake and bower,
Along the solitary vale,
Where sang the cheering nightingale ?
His form was of athletic mould,
His step was stately, firm and bold,
A martial style of dress he wore,
His belt a long-tried rapier bore,
A helm of steel enclosed his head,
Above it waving plumes of red;
And though the day had long since flown,
He wore his visor closely down ;
For he was bent on deeds of shame,
Though rank and lineage might he claim.
'Twas dark Sir Lockwell, fierce and stern,
Whose heart could naught of kindness learn,
Whose bosom burned with vengeful ire,
If crossed in any one desire ;
And he had many times essayed
To win the hand of Moran's maid.
But she to falsehood aye unused,
His offers honestly refused ;
Ill brooking which, his evil mind
At once a base revenge designed ;
And as by Conyard's cot he sped,
More cautious there became his tread,
As though he feared to break the rest
Of those in happy slumbers blest:
Then went he hastily along,
Far down the moon-lit vale of Tong ;
And many a copse and stream he passed,

Until Park-Springs was reached at last,
Which in those times of strife and fear
Was all romantic, wild, and drear ;
No human dwellings then, I ween,
Destroyed the sweetness of the scene ;
Where now the mill pours forth its smoke,
Then rolled the little babbling brook ;
Soft beds of flowers adorned the spot,
And many a woodbine-covered grot.
The stranger there a moment stood,
Then plunged into the silent wood,
Whose full blown foliage calmly hung
And deeper gloom around him flung ;
Here dark and darker shadows grew,
There moonbeams faintly flickered through,
Forming such scenes as might impart
Fair subjects for the painter's art,
Or scenes from which the bard might draw
Bright inspiration, touched with awe.
But that bold man regarded not
The charms of this enchanting spot ;
He saw no beauty in the sky,
The fairest tree gave him no joy,
He felt no bliss in darksome shades,
He found no love in flowery glades ;
His thoughts in other channels ran,
Concocting many a graceless plan.
His devious way he still pursued,
'Mid calm and glorious solitude,
Now climbing up a steep ascent,
Next down a winding path he went,

Through many a dark and cooling glade,
Where intersecting brambles spread;
Until at length far in the wood,
Deep in a dingle green he stood,
Where many paths turned various ways
By thorny brake and thickening maze.
Not long he paused, but stepping on
—For well each track to him seemed known—
He turned him towards the Rankling Stone,
Which, scowling in the shades of night,
Seemed like a giant in its might,
Rearing its dark majestic form,
As if defying fire or storm:
Rude craggy steeps had he to tread,
Ere he could reach its dusky head;
With wearying step he journeyed on
The seldom trodden footpath lone,
While Cynthia's soft and silvery light
Shewed him to scan the Rankling's height,
And after a fatiguing climb
He sat upon its brow sublime;
Some moments stayed he resting there,
To breathe the sweet refreshing air.
On that huge rock, when Sol rode high,
I've stood and felt a boundless joy,
To view the wide expansive scene
Of waving woods and meadows green;
Fair hills where modest flowerets grow,
The silent vale deep sunk below;
Where murmuring brooklets turn and twine,
And all like molten silver shine;

While in the distance, miles away,
Are mansions seen and hamlets grey :
I'd travel twenty miles alone,
Again to view the Rankling Stone !
Not so with him, the stranger knight,
Who there reclined that silent night ;
No tender throb his bosom swelled,
His eye no glorious scenes beheld ;
He saw not in the stars on high
Ten thousand gems of poesy ;
The place, the hour, gave him no bliss,
For dark and morbid thoughts were his.
With plots of guilt his mind was fraught,
And there a well tried friend he sought ;
One who was born to wealth and pride,
But had in youth that wealth destroyed :
An early gamester he became,
By which he won disgrace and shame,
And driven to despair and need,
Committed many a fearful deed ;
Which proved to him sufficient cause
To flee the vengeance of the laws ;
And in those woods, with altered name,
He thus an outlaw-wretch became,
And shortly had at his command
A truly bold and dauntless band,
Who heeded not their nation's woe,
Nor cared how human blood might flow ;
Nor heeded they the widow's wail,
Nor orphan's tear, nor love-lorn tale ;
But took advantage of the times

c

To stain their hands with deepest crimes.
Such were the men 'midst woodlands free,
Whose chief Sir Lockwell came to see;
For they on terms of friendship were,
Made strong with many a by-gone year;
Full oft in plots of guilt they'd shared,
Ere he—the chief—his wealth impaired;
Had often joined the midnight glee
Of riot and of revelry;
And oft had Lockwell sought his aid,
Since in the woods his home was made.
Thus came he now, nor came in vain,
To ask Hugh Lenard's aid again;
And midnight reigned and bright stars shone,
As turned he from the Rankling Stone.
Then stepping onward to the right,
Along the thickly wooded height,
An open space he soon did gain
Which might a hundred men contain.
'Twas there the robbers held their home,
Where undescried no foe might come;
For on the right deep valleys lie,
The left, dark rocks are towering high;
None then could gain that wild abode,
Save by the path that Lockwell trod,
Who crossed with slow and stately stride
The glen that nears its rock-bound side;
When a deep voice fell on his ear,
Exclaiming sternly " Who goes there?"
" A friend," our traveller replied;
" Thy name," the other quickly cried.

" It boots thee naught my name to know,
Be proud that I am not thy foe."
" Nay marry, proud i' faith, not I,"
Was the bold sentinel's reply ;
" For, by my trust, I fear not thee,
Though lord or baron thou may'st be ;
And learn, sir, ere thou leav'st this spot,
Thou giv'st thy name or leav'st it not."
The speaker was robust in limb,
With features scowling, dark and grim ;
A fiery, quick and restless eye,
That flashed and twinkled scornfully ;
A broad belt buckled round his waist
With dagger there and pistols placed ;
And paced he 'fore a yawning cave
With brawny arm and naked glaive ;
And him Sir Lockwell keenly eyed
With feelings strong of wounded pride ;
Who thus addressed the guard again,
In measured tones of high disdain :
" Insensate ruffian, basely bred,
Unworthy of my trusty blade,
Else would I smite thee where thou art,
And trample on thy knavish heart.
But words I bandy not with thee,
My business is thy chief to see ;
Go straight to him, my message bear,
And say a friend awaits him here ;
One who his presence will deserve,
And one whom he'll be proud to serve."
" Nay, by the mass", the robber cried,

And laughed aloud at Lockwell's pride ;
" I ask no favour at thy hand,
Nor quit my post at thy command,
Nor to my captain word will say ;
For none but him do I obey."
This filled the knight with angry fire
And swelled him with indignant ire.
" Stand off," he cried, " And have a care,
Myself will to thy chief repair."
" Hold !" was the other's quick reply ;
" One step advance, and thou shalt die ;
Seek not to enter this our cave,
Or thy heart's blood my sword shall lave."
And as he spake his weapon fell
'Gainst that of Lockwell wielded well,
The flashing blades with horrid clang
Upon the midnight silence rang ;
And from the cavern of the glen
Soon issued strong and desperate men,
With broad swords gleaming in the air,
And pistols charged, and daggers bare.
But ere they shed each other's blood,
The daring captain betwixt them stood ;
" Hold, on your life," he cried, " Forbear !
How comes this midnight clamour here ?
Who first shall strike another blow,
His blood shall o'er my rapier flow."
But as he spake, his rolling eye
Observed the bold knight standing by ;
And at that hour much wondered he
A visored stranger there to see,

Alone and in his stronghold too,
Contending with his followers true.
" Who art thou, wretch ?" he fiercely said,
And waved the steel above his head ;
" The cause of thy intrusion give
Or little time thou hast to live."
" Be cool, good Hugh," the knight exclaimed,
'· My errand here may soon be named."
At once he dropped the lifted blade
Which soon was in its scabbard laid ;
He knew the voice that struck his ear, ⎫
And turning to the bravoes near, ⎬
He motioned all to disappear,— ⎭
Who soon were lost in caverns deep,
Their midnight revels there to keep,—
Then said, " Sir knight, I much mistake,
If 'twas not Lockwell's self that spake ;
Come, come, put up thy rapier now,
Undo thy mask and bare thy brow,
And let me see thee face to face ;
Fear not in this secluded place."
The knight at once his friend obeyed,
As with a scornful smile he said,
" Those braggart dogs of thine, I ween,
Have surely sprung from kennels mean,
Who growl and ope' their grisly jaws,
And show their fangs without a cause.
'Twere well thou savedst my furious foe,
Or soon my arm had laid him low."
" Aye, aye," the robber chief rejoined,
" Those dogs unflinching friends I find,

Ready to serve me at a word,
With willing arm and trusty sword
To do whatever I may say,
And e'en my glance or nod obey.
Call them base dogs or what you will,
But seek not, sir, their blood to spill ;
I would not change this little band
For all the knights in this broad land.
And should'st thou have more errand here,
To give thee passage safe and clear,
Accept in friendship this small ring ;
'Twill save mistakes and combating,
Which to my brave companions known,
Shall be thy passport duly shown.
And now thy business,—come, begin ;
Say, sir, what I may serve thee in,
For well I know thy journey here
Does sign of some importance bear."
" My purpose, Hugh, thou soon shalt find
Is of an interesting kind ;
Yet wilt thou deem me weak to say
My heart is pierced by lady gay."
" I'faith, not I, for well I know
Thy heart has oft been wounded so ;
Well cans't thou ply the rowelled heel,
Or turn the foeman's deadly steel,
But cans't not ward the dart that flies
From lovely woman's witching eyes.
Myself have known you love a score,
And then perhaps a hundred more."
" Aye, true, but this is one most fair.

Nay smile not, Hugh, for now I swear
By all around, below, above,
She seems created but for love.
The light that lives in her sweet eye
Flings forth excess of ecstasy ;
And such a form thou ne'er hast seen—
Fairer than any fabled queen ;
Her tresses of a darkish brown
Like finest silk flow softly down,
And play upon a bosom rife
With all a virgin's warmth and life.
But ah ! that bosom does contain
A heart replete with high disdain ;
My proffered hand she proudly spurns,
And for my love but scorn returns.
Full well thou knowest I ne'er could brook
A lady's scornful word or look ;
And by my falchion's edge, I swear,
I'll have, perforce, this haughty fair,
And make her, though she slight me still,
At once subservient to my will.
I'd body risk, and risk the soul,
The wealthy damsel to control."
" Perhaps," observed the captain, " she
To other lord betrothed may be."
" Nay," interrupted Lockwell, " Nay,
Not so, I dare be sworn to say ;
No other suitor has the maid,
By all the saints ! and if she had
He soon should lie amongst the dead.
Her father, true to glory's call,

Short time ago left his strong hall,
To join the royal ranks in fight,
To guard the monarch and his right ;
But ere he donned his coat of steel,
Or buckled rowel to his heel,
A guardian for his child he sought,
And her to Conyard's cottage brought,
Which hence not half a league doth lie,
With not another dwelling nigh ;
Deeming her safe in this lone vale,
Should rebel bands his hall assail ;
And 'tis her wont, by twilight grey,
Among the neighbouring woods to stray,
And softly sing her evening lay."
" I've heard her oft," the captain said,
" And, faith, sir knight, if she's the maid,
You yield her not the praises due ;
Of gallant knight or lover true,
A voice so truly sweet has ne'er
Before flung rapture on the ear :
Mine eyes ne'er saw so fair a flower
In lordly hall or lady's bower ;
And marry, sir, good truth to say,
When I have journeyed on that way,
I have been tempted oft to go,
And on my knee the charmer woo.
The woodlands green she seems to love,
And here at pleasure might she rove,
Or safely lie when tempests rave
Within our storm-defying cave.
But blame me not, for I resign

That thought, since thou would'st have her thine."
Sir Lockwell scowled, and his dark eye
Shot darts of doubt and jealousy;
But Lenard's closing words at once
Inspired him with fresh confidence;
And, casting off the gathering gloom,
His orders he did thus resume:
" Captain, I would with thy kind aid
Have yonder lady captive made;
A couple of thy trusty men
Might easy bear her to this glen;
And two nights hence, at this same hour,
I'd take her to my highest tower,
Where none but I might ever dare
Approach her secret home to share.
Myself had borne away the prize,
But fearing Conyard's watchful eyes,
Who knows me well and might straightway
To Moran's lord the news convey;
By which upon my name and hall
A stigma of disgrace would fall.
But if the maid were once but here,
I might conduct her, free from fear
Of that old guardian's cautious eye,
Unto my turrets firm and high.
Befriend me, Hugh, without delay,
And fullest recompense I'll pay;
Thou need'st not thy reward to name,
For gold uncounted shalt thou claim.
But still my name and rank must be
A secret held to all but thee."

" 'Tis well," the captain said, " depend,
Forthwith to-morrow night we'll send
Two daring men who shall not fail
To bring the lady from the vale.
I'll lodge her well till thou shalt come
To take her to her destined home ;
Nor need'st thou e'en to doubt incline,
But deem the maid already thine."
" Enough my friend," rejoined the knight ;
" Thy service I shall well requite ;
To-morrow, at this hour, believe
No mean reward shalt thou receive :
Till then, farewell ! be firm, be true."
" Doubt not," the captain said, " Adieu."
 Thus parted they who thus combined
Against a maiden's peace of mind.
Hugh Lenard sought his rock-bound hold,
To muse o'er Lockwell's promised gold ;
While he again with visor on
Soon stood upon the Rankling Stone ;
Then down the dangerous steep he made
With slow but firm and cautious tread,
And soon 'midst woodlands glooming grey
Did he retrace his former way ;
And oft he muttered " Now, proud dame !
Thy charms I will not woo, but claim ;
Now will I quell thy boundless pride,
And make thee mine though not my bride.
Shall Lockwell's knight a truant run
From bold design when onee begun ?
No, never shall he swerve or change,

Till he has reaped a full revenge.
Each hope of heaven, or fear of hell,
Would I defy, her pride to quell;
To make her with a tear-stained cheek
My late disdained affections seek.
Then with what pride should I return
Her stern rejection and her scorn."
Thus journeying by the moon's pale beam,
He fondly cherished this wild dream;
His morbid spirit swelled, replete
With dark revenge and foul deceit.

And this was passing that same night
When Rosco's dreams were of delight;
That night on which he'd wondering stood,
Had seen fair Lucia·in the wood,
And listened to her voice so rare,
So rich and mellow to the ear.
And 'twas on that next following day,—
When Rosco wished for twilight grey
That he might see that form again,
And hear once more the witching strain—
That Lockwell also deeply sighed
For darksome shades of eventide;
And fancy pictured to his eyes
The bravoes bearing off the prize;
While on his longing ears did seem
To fall the frighted ·victim's scream,
When greatest pleasures he enjoyed
O'er innocence and worth destroyed.
Thus sitting in his mansion gay,

He mused and wiled the time away;
While Rosco at his home obscure
Could ill the lengthy day endure;
But different far his thoughts inclined
To those of Lockwell's guilty mind.
He only wished, he scarce knew why,
That gentle even would draw nigh;
He wished once more to hear the voice,
That made his very soul rejoice,
And once again that form to see
Of such unmatched transcendancy.
  Meantime the captain of the cave
That day the needful orders gave
And chose two men, a ruthless pair,
To capture Moran's daughter fair.
And Lucia never dreamed the while
Of Rosco's love or Lockwell's guile,
Nor deemed how danger forth might stalk
And lurk upon her evening walk.
No; her young artless breast was fraught
With only one absorbing thought;
The welfare of her noble sire
Was all her hope, her sole desire;
For him her prayers devoutly given
Each night were warmly breathed to heaven.
Then with the harp she'd forth again,
And yield the woods a pensive strain;
All gentle, mild and nought afraid,
Roamed Moran's unsuspecting maid.

END OF CANTO SECOND.

CANTO THIRD.

Far over heaven's broad expanse
Bright Sol had shed his parting glance,
And rolled far west his god-like eye,
In grandeur and in majesty,
To spread his never-dying beams
O'er other lands and other streams,
To yield his bounteous favours then
To other thankless sons of men.
The moon resumed her wonted reign,
High in the boundless space again ;
A myriad stars illumed the sky,
And held the fair queen company:
When youthful Rosco slowly strayed
Once more beneath the green-wood shade,
Hoping the maid would wander out
And rid his mind of every doubt.
But lest his presence might annoy
Her walk, or make her backward fly,
He sought in dingle deep to hide
Where he might not be well descried,
And thus in secret ambuscade
Await the passing of the maid ;
Who soon appeared on dewy lawn,
With footsteps lighter than the fawn.
She slowly came along the way
Close by the brambles where he lay,
So close he might have touched with ease
Her garments rustling by the trees ;

Then was he tempted forth to stand
And woo the wondrous fair one's hand ;
But modesty that thought dispelled,
And still the secret place he held;
For not a hope his heart could move,
Save that of pure unsullied love ;
And gazing on the gentle form
He felt his bosom waxing warm ;
A sacred flame was kindled there
Which nought but death could e'er impair ;
His blood ran quick and hope rose high
And throbbed his heart in ecstasy.
But Lucia slowly moved along,
Till lost the shady trees among,
And soon on Rosco's listening ear
Her harp strings sounded soft and clear ;
At first the notes were incomplete,
And broken oft, but passing sweet;
As if each sep'rate chord she tried
With all a careful minstrel's pride;
Then swelling to a full sweet air,—
Thus joined with it the guileless fair.

SONG.

Pretty warbler, O ! come near me,
  Yielding thy harmonious tale,
Not another bird can cheer me,
  Like thyself, sweet nightingale !
      Now no sounds but thine intrude,
      Little bird of solitude.

Why are thy soft lays imparted
  When thy tuneful kindred rest ;
Has thy heart with sorrow smarted,
  Can a grief disturb thy breast?
      Sure thou know'st not troubles rude,
      Lovely bird of solitude.

Thou dost charm the woodlands lonely,
  When the night is gathering drear,
Pouring forth thy cadence only
  When no others reach the ear ;
      Night by night thy song 's renewed,
      Gentle bird of solitude.

Larks and linnets carol loudly,
  When refulgent day beams shine ;
Finch and black-cap whistle proudly,
  But their songs ne'er equal thine,
      Falling on this quietude,
      Cheering bird of solitude.

Thy sweet notes can soothe the sadness
  Of the heart to grief consigned,
And afford bright rays of gladness
  To the melancholy mind ;
      Thou art heard but rarely viewed,
      Lonesome bird of solitude.

When the twilight round is closing,
  And the stars of heaven appear ;
When the winds lie still reposing,
  O, I love to wander here,
      Where no sounds but thine intrude,
      Light-toned bird of solitude.

Softly away the gentle cadence died,
Like the sweet whispers of the bashful bride ;
And for some moments silence deep prevailed,
No rising sound his 'wildered ear assailed.
  But hark ! that wild and startling scream
Which echoes over wood and stream—
'Twas surely Lucia's voice that rang,
As Rosco from his covert sprang,
From scabbard snatching his short blade
To lend—if need required—his aid :
That piercing scream arose again,
And dashed he on the path she'd ta'en,
And soon descried through shadows grey
Two ruffians bearing her away,
Who hurried on through dell and brake
With all the speed they well could make.
In him his father's soul rose high,
And gen'rous fire lit up his eye,
While indignation filled his breast
To see the maiden rudely prest;
And on he went like warrior brave
To perish by her or to save.
Like the swift stag when dogs give need,

He bounded on with utmost speed,
And, ere the knaves were scarce aware,
One hand was on the fainting fair,
The other raised ;—in accents bold
He cried, " Base caitiffs, quit your hold !
Ye treacherous slaves, who thus assail
A helpless maid in lonesome vale ;
Perfidious curs ! who thus betray
Unguarded innocence, away !
Back, cowards, back ! or ye may feel
The force of this my honest steel:
Unhand her, or by all that's good
My weapon's point shall drink your blood."
The astonished bravoes darkly scowled,
Their burning eyes on Rosco rolled :
" Rash youth," the stouter said, " Beware !
'Twere well those insults thou should'st spare,
Lest I should crush thee with a blow,
And leave thee to the carrion crow :
Hence, madman, tempt me not so near,
Hence, fool, and leave our passage clear.
" Never," replied the noble youth,
" I quit you not, by my good sooth ;
Ere ye the affrighted maid shall bear
Another single step, I swear,
By all yon splendid host on high,
Myself or both of you shall die."
" Then die," the other hoarsely cried,
And aimed a thrust at Rosco's side,
Who turned the blow with dexterous hand,
And plied his own unsullied brand ;

D

His arm was strong, his weapon light,
But all unknown to actual fight;
Yet well the sire his son had taught
To fight as he himself had fought:
The robber tried his utmost skill,
But all was ineffectual still;
With growing ire he struck again,
But found his every effort vain;
Each point and pass he often tried,
And each as oft was turned aside:
As oft the gallant Rosco could
Have shed the desp'rate traitor's blood;
But though he joined him in the strife,
He wished not, sought not, for his life;
His only care was to repel
The blows that from his foeman fell.
Meantime the hapless Lucia lay
Like lifeless and unconscious clay;
The other wretch with glaring eyes
Stood watchful o'er their gentle prize,
And once advanced his aid to lend
And put the contest to an end:
But " No," the other fiercely cried,
" Ourselves this combat will decide:
Stand off, the blows are short and few
That shall this beardless fool subdue."
Then sprang he full upon his foe,
Intending one decisive blow;
But Rosco, firm as granite rock,
Smiled and received the heavy shock,
And harmless still the stroke was turned,

While many a foot the wretch was spurned;
Who stood aghast and wildly gazed,
With Rosco's art and strength amazed,
And thought, as he our friend did scan,
" 'Tis surely something more than man ;
Yet whatsoe'er thou art," he cried,
" Once more my weapon shall be plied."
But stepping out the youth to meet,
A straggling bramble caught his feet,
And cast him headlong, while his brand
Flew forth from his exhausted hand :
The partner of his guilt had seen
Our hero's strength, and, well I ween,
Had no desire to tempt his might,
 And so betook himself to flight;
While Rosco with uplifted blade
Unto the prostrate bravo said :
"Now, dastard wretch, thy life, thy blood
Is in my hands, if such I would;
But much I'd scorn my sword to stain
 With streams from such a caitiff's vein ;
Else long ere now 't had been my part
To dash my rapier through thy heart.
Rise villain, rise, and get thee gone;
Say to the churl who set thee on
This vile attempt, whoe'er he be,
That banished Rosco's son is free
To give him fight for insult played
Upon a young and harmless maid.
Hence, traitor, hence, my presence flee,

Lest tempted yet my arm may be
To crush thee with thy own foul glaive,
A meed thou well deserv'st to have."
  As baffled tiger hastes away,
When disappointed of his prey;
As thief skulks off at midnight drear,
When watchdog's bark assails his ear;
So sneaked he off without reply,
Abashed 'neath Rosco's piercing eye,
Who, turning, kind assistance gave
To her his arm had serv'd to save.
And pale she stood as Cynthia's beam,
Like one just roused from fearful dream;
She'd seen disarmed the robber lie,
And marked her champion standing by;
She'd heard him speak, and breathe his name,
And knew 'twas one of knightly fame;
Full oft had known her father tell,
How Rosco's lance the foe could quell;
How he had basked a goodly while
Beneath a fickle monarch's smile;
How, by the hand that had caressed,
He had from high estate been cast,
And how his pride was wounded then,
And fled he from the haunts of men:
Full well she guessed to look upon
Her saviour as that Rosco's son.
" Permit me, gentle maid," he sighed,
" From this lone grove to be thy guide,
To guard thee home, where'er it be,

And lead thee from all dangers free."
With downcast eye and blushing cheek,
Oft did her lips essay to speak ;
But virgin modesty suppressed
As oft the wish of her young breast.
At length with trembling breath she said,
" Most noble youth, for thy kind aid
A world of thanks would only be
A mark of veriest mockery ;
But Moran's lord shall well reward
Him who has deigned his child to guard."
" Lady," again her friend exclaimed,
" Let no reward or thanks be named
To him who flies at virtue's call,
And yields his aid alike to all:
Hadst thou another maiden been,
A peasant girl or royal queen,
My efforts had been lent the same
To guard thee 'gainst a traitor's aim:
No thanks are due, save those to Heaven,
By Whom the will and power is given ;
And yet, believe, right proud am I
At having been prepared and nigh,
To rescue Moran's only child
And keep her beauties undefiled.
But, maiden, what could serve to call
Thy presence from a lordly hall,
Unwatched, unguarded, thus to dwell
In this remote and silent vale ?
I marvel much in times like these,
How thou canst here sojourn at ease ;

Methinks thy father's ancient tower
Were better shield in danger's hour.
A bright tear sprung to Lucia's eye,
As thus she made a brief reply :—
" Some time ago my loving sire
In haste put on his steel attire,
And, vaulting to his steed of war,
Sped off to scenes of broil and jar ;
And thought me safe in this retreat
From rebel bands or foul deceit :
Alas ! but little does he trow
How enemies beset me now."
   By this (on that advent'rous night)
The humble cot appeared in sight,
Without whose porch the Conyards stood,
With anxious eyes turned to the wood ;
For long their ward had been away,
And much they wondered at her stay ;
Nor less, indeed, amazed they were
To see with her a stranger there.
Then Lucia straight began to tell,
How into dangerous hands she fell ;
And how the stranger at her side
Her base assailants had defied ;
And how he had the foes subdued,
And snatched her from the ruffians rude.
Her guardian gazed, as if in fear
That danger still might hover near,
Then bent upon the youth his eyes
In admiration and surprise.
The moon's chaste beams were softly thrown,

Which full on Rosco's features shone ;
And Conyard looked with eye intent
On him in deep bewilderment,
And seemed he as he'd recognized
Some long lost friend he dearly prized ;
A lowly bow he then did make,
And thus unto the stranger spake:—
" Courageous youth, I scarcely know
How my heart's gratitude to show ;
Such daring act so nobly done
Our lasting love and thanks has won !
He who has wrought so bold a deed
Must surely spring of knightly breed ;
It may, perchance, beseem him not
To honour so our lowly cot,
Else gladly would I have him come
Short time within our humble home ;
But rank and fame, I much deplore,
Too oft despise the lowly poor."
As Conyard spoke of rank and fame,
A cloud o'er Rosco's features came,
A darksome cloud of pensive gloom,
As thinking of his former home,
And of his aged father's fall
From high estate and spacious hall ;
And in his bosom warm and young,
Arose emotions wild and strong,
Emotions he could ill restrain,
As calmly thus he spake again :—
" Most truly, good and worthy sage,
The deep respect we owe to age

Should well suffice to cast aside
Each other thought of pomp and pride;
Gay youth, in whatsoe'er degree,
Might rev'rence age where'er it be ;
In hall or hut of every land,
White hairs our kindness still command;
And proud am I that 'tis my lot
A guest to be within thy cot.
Methinks our king might deign to grace
With his great self so sweet a place,
Where age and peace and love reside,
Amid fair Nature's bloom and pride.
No hero I of knightly fame,
No champion of reputed name ;
But were I such, 'twould glad my breast
To be of thine a constant guest,
To dwell where flowers grow sweet and wild,
And guard brave Moran's lovely child."
As thus he spake, he heaved a sigh,
And sought a glance of Lucia's eye,
As if he said, " Fair maid would you,
Accept me as thy champion true?"
The blushing maiden hung her head,
But nothing in response essayed ;
Yet her young soul was beating high
With true love's brightest ecstasy :
That soul, so gentle and so young,
To her deliverer fondly clung,
And, though she could not bid him stay,
His going she would still delay ;
The wily god had cast the dart,

And thrown his meshes round her heart ;
And who that love misplaced shall deem
On one so worthy her esteem ?
Moreover, Rosco's graceful form
Possessed in full each manly charm ;
Warm rosy hues were on his cheek
Which did a healthy frame bespeak ;
The glance of his dark eye expressed
The gen'rous nature of his breast ;
A forehead lofty, broad and fair,
Bedecked with dark luxuriant hair ;
In short a handsome youth was he,
As lady e'er might wish to see.
And Conyard, with solicitous care,
Bade him a thousand welcomes there,
Then, turning without more delay,
Into the cottage led the way.
Its neat interior seemed to tell
What sweet contentment there might dwell ;
Its furniture, though passing old,
Was bright as any burnished gold ;
The oaken chest, the ancient chair,
Like clean and spotless mirrors were.
The old man trimmed the lamp apace,
Whose rays danced cheerly round the place ;
Then looked he full in Rosco's face,
And doubt and hope and wonder prest
In conflict through his aged breast ;
And long his anxious gaze was bent,
As studying every lineament :
Once turned he pale, then his dim eye

Became illumed with sudden joy;
Our dauntless hero's hand he grasped,
And long within his own held clasped,
Then cried, in an impassioned tone,—
" Thou'rt, sure, my once brave master's son!
It must be so, his features shine
In every changing glance of thine :
Speak, say, brave sir, in sooth declare,
Art thou not noble Rosco's heir."
" 'Tis even so," was the reply
Delivered with a mournful sigh ;
The old man's wrinkled face grew bright,
As if in transports of delight.
" O," he exclaimed, " how proud I'd be
Once more thy father's form to see,
Whom long I served in days gone by,
When thou wert yet a thoughtless boy;
His was a tender heart and brave,
As ever noble nature gave.
I've known him, in the forest chase,
Confront the bold wolf face to face ;
I've seen him on the battle field,
The trusty axe and broad sword wield ;
At home that warrior have I seen
Calm as the lamb that nips the green,
Dispensing favours round his hall,
Beloved by his retainers all.
But fickle fortune's changing tide
With sudden shift its smiles denied,
And from that time I ne'er could learn
Where it has pleased him to sojourn;

Else long ere now I had been there,
To see the knight I still revere."
" Truly my friend," the youth rejoined,
" Thy speech bespeaks a nature kind ;
But much I fear thou ne'er can'st gaze
Again on him thou yield'st such praise :
Though not far distant from this spot
He dwells, as 'twere by all forgot,
Few are our friends, our mansion small,
And strangers seem we still to all ;
Under a name assumed we live,
And none our actual rank conceive :
My injured Sire, in silent grief,
Ne'er seeks in change of scene relief ;
But 'neath a deeply settled gloom
He mourns, and seldom leaves his home ;
And age and direful trouble now
Have stamped their marks upon his brow.
Methinks grim death will shortly close
The term of all his earthly woes."
O'er Conyard's cheek rolled burning tears,
As such sad tidings reached his ears.
And now ensued a silence brief,
As he was venting forth his grief ;
While that brave youth and lady fair
Exchanged a thousand glances there ;
Such glances as might serve to move
The sternest soul to terms of love ;
For each the other's heart might claim,
Though still untold the tender flame,
Save by the cheek of crimson dye,

Or that clear language of the eye
Which can such deep emotions wake,
And silent, soft confessions make.
And well the dame, who watched with care,
Could read the looks of that young pair,
Much fearing lest their love might err,
And thus lord Moran's wrath incur ;
For deemed she that her ward should mate
With noble earl of high estate,
And not with one who could not claim
A title to adorn her name.

Again the old man raised his head,
And looking up to Rosco, said,
" Alas, brave youth, I much deplore
That I must see thy sire no more ;
But thou perchance wilt deign to come
By times unto our humble home,
That we at least may often hear
Of him my memory still holds dear."
" Freely I would," was his reply,
" But may not with thy wish comply ;
For much my heart has yearned of late
On battle field to try my fate :
My father's will, but yesterday,
Commanded I should haste away,
To seek 'gainst the rebellious foe
That rank he cannot now bestow :
But, ere I leave my aged sire,
And from these happy scenes retire,
I'd gladly first this lady see

In some place of security ;
For treachery is lurking nigh,
And danger and calamity."

At this suggestion seemed to rise
The old man's failing energies :
" Yes," he replied, " by my good faith,
Conyard would rather meet his death,
Than aught of evil should betide
Lord Moran's lovely hope and pride ;
And shortly shall the gentle fair
Straightway to Lumbley Hall repair,
Whose owners loyal are and true,
And Lucia's loving kinsmen too ;
Where first her father did design
To leave this priceless charge of mine,
But feared he such a lordly hall
Would prove a mark for foeman's ball."
" Such sad result, indeed, might be,"
The other said ; " but surely she
Were better in rebellious hands,
Than dragged away by midnight bands :
And true it is that some vile snare
Is placed for her with subtle care ;
But why—or who the wretch may be,
Seems wrapped as yet in mystery."
" True," Conyard cried ; " No time to spare,
To morrow she must all prepare ;
And, early on the following day,
To Lumbley she shall speed away.
Fear not my fair, my honoured ward,

Myself will be thy guide and guard ;
And though my limbs be stiff with years,
And hung my brow with snowy hairs,
Yet well, methinks, I still could wield
A sword thy beauteous self to shield."
The maid was mute, but her bright eye
Her guardian thanked full earnestly ;
Right proud was she such friends to have,
So truly noble and so brave.
Our hero rose to take his leave,
While much the lady's heart did grieve ;
For her fond breast with fear was rife
Lest some one should assail his life,
And felt his loss she could not bear,
Already was he held so dear.
Albeit a warm adieu she sighed,
And strove in vain her love to hide ;
For Rosco read in her bright eyes
A thousand hopes of tender joys.
Again the old man fondly prest
The hand of his unlooked for guest,
Who promised, as he bade adieu, ·
His visit shortly to renew,
And gracefully his head was bent
To all as from the cot he went ;
Then homeward turned with quickening speed,
Well pleased with his first gallant deed.

Her couch lord Moran's daughter sought,
Her breast with joy and wonder fraught,
For much perplexed was she to know

Who had become her lurking foe ;
Yet proud she was that such event
Had thus a noble champion sent :
So well had Lockwell played his part,
That Lucia's inexperienced heart
Ne'er once suspected that proud knight
Could e'er have wished her peace to blight.
O'er many a guess and vain surmise
She mused, till slumber closed her eyes.

END OF CANTO THIRD.

CANTO FOURTH.

'Twas at that hour when Rosco hied
Along the vale with heartfelt pride,
A scene, which we must here unfold,
Transpired within the robber's hold.
Deep in the cave a spacious room,
Whose lamps did but enhance its gloom,
Was filled with men who knew no fear,
Whose features dark and sullen were,
Denoting hearts wild, stern and bold,
Whose faith was blood, whose god was gold.
Through that uncouth apartment ran
A table on the rudest plan,

On which were bottles, cups of horn,
And swords, in many a conflict borne;
All sat save two, who were the men
Dispatched, from that romantic glen,
To bring the maid of many charms
Unto the worthless Lockwell's arms,
And who had just returned replete
With fierce chagrin at their defeat,
To tell how they had seized the maid,
And how their progress had been stayed
By one who but a stripling seemed,
But whom they now a monster deemed;
How they had fought the prize to gain,
But every effort proved in vain;
That every pass and blow they made
Was turned as if by magic aid;
Concluding with deep marks of shame,
And Rosco's challenge and his name.
When this was told, the captain's blood
Rushed round his heart an angry flood;
His eyes, each like a living fire,
Bespoke his bosom's stirring ire;
And, starting from his seat, he strode
About the cave in desperate mood;
While silent there was every tongue,
Mute as the craggs that o'er them hung:
Then moved his lips with scornful curl;—
" What foiled in gaining yon weak girl!
And challenged too by some vain boy,
Who doubtless woos the lady's eye;
And he to brave such men as you,

Whom I had deemed my boldest two !
By hell ! 'tis false beyond compare.
Ye sneaking dogs, ye coward pair,
May fiends and furies rise to night
And drag you from my loathing sight.
'Twere well were ye ere morning thrown
Both headlong from the Rankling Stone;
There left, that vermin of the vale
Might on your craven hearts regale.
What ! have ye tongues to say ye fought
And struggled for the prize ye'd caught,
When not a stain of blood ye show
To prove the prowess of your foe ?
Go, tell me not,—'tis false, 'tis base,
Your conduct does our bands disgrace.
Had I myself once grasped the fair,
Though hell and all its hosts were there,
I would have held them bloody strife,
And won my charge or lost my life.
Ye merit not a brave man's death,
Or in your hearts my sword I'd sheath."
And, as this threat the captain made,
Toward their breasts he thrust his blade ;
And those fierce men, who feared but few, ⎫
Shrunk back as Lenard nearer drew ; ⎬
For well his heated wrath they knew. ⎭
And long he foamed and long he raged,
Like a wild lion newly caged ;
At length again resumed his seat,
And muttered oft, " A foul defeat !"
His broad chest heaved and sank amain,

E

As though 'twas nigh to burst in twain.
Often the foaming wine he quaffed,
Imbibing many a copious draught;
As oft his gaze, with fearful glare,
Was turned on the defeated pair,
Who stood and quailed beneath his eye,
Like culprits just condemned to die :
Then from his seat once more he sprang,
And thus addressed the daring gang :
" Mansford and Jones, and gallant Ray,
Seize these two knaves without delay,
Conduct them to the deepest cell,
And bar them close and watch them well;
For, by my troth, there seems to be
In their report some treachery.
How might these men, who oft have been
Assailed with double strength, I ween,
Be conquered by a paltry boy,
And scarless thus be made to fly ?
'Tis most absurd, and well shall they
The forfeit of their baseness pay.
Saunders, and nine of you, prepare
To guard our entrance now with care ;
And, honest Sedley, thou alone
Keep watch upon the Rankling Stone ;
And shouldst thou aught that way descry,
Straight to the glen with warning fly ;
Such welcome shall the dogs receive
As vultures to the lambkins give.
The rest of our brave men shall lie,
Ready their trusty swords to ply :—

Our pass-word now we must exchange
For that of ' Lenard and Revenge'—
And thus prepared our force will be
For any dire emergency."

Each party of the dauntless band
Passed to their posts at his command;
While he, with pistols at his belt,
And dagger, many a breast had felt,
Upon his arm his falchion bore,
And thus he paced the cavern floor.
But often in the midst he stood,
As in a deeply musing mood,
And, often starting, gazed around,
As though he heard the signal sound;
At times he'd to his seat return,
And quaff a brimmer from the horn.
Thus passed the heavy hours away,
Till far into the following day
The sun his noontide heights had cleared;
But nothing hostile had appeared.
All undisturbed the woodlands lay,
No zephyrs moved the lightest spray,
While sweetest harmony was heard
From many a little heedless bird,
Its breast from every trouble free,
Suspicion, fear or treachery;
Unlike vain man, whose dreamy life
Is one continued scene of strife;
Whate'er his fortune or degree,
Still discontented must he be;

Whate'er his wealth or worldly store,
He daily seeks and grasps at more,
Thus wasting useful time to gain
The thing he cannot long retain,
Neglecting all the bliss refined
That nature giveth to mankind.
The simple feathered tribes enjoy
The soft green meads, the forests high;
They build their nests with artful care,
And nature's brightest treasures share;
Thus all delighted pass their days
In singing thé Creator's praise:
While man, who boasts a higher stand,
The noblest work of Nature's hand,
Is ever at dispute and jar,
All scenes of peace and love to mar,
Each hour conceiving some new plan
To rob and crush his fellow-man.

Another eve drew nigh apace,
And still the watchmen kept their place,
By turns retiring to the cave
Refreshment or repose to have:
The hours rolled on, the broad moon rose,
But brought not still their fancied foes;
The glistening stars, in splendour bright,
Lent sweetness to the gloom of night.
That night dark Lockwell was to come,
And claim the prize and bear it home;
To take the lovely jewel forth,
And rob it of its purest worth;

To triumph o'er a treasure rare,
Obtained by foul and treacherous snare.
And midnight came—that solemn hour,
When ghosts are said to haunt each tower;
And all was silent, save the brawl
Of neighbouring brook or waterfall;
Or now and then the broad deep vale
Rang with the owl's discordant wail;
All else in slumber seemed to lie,
The fair green earth, the boundless sky.

Anon, a human form drew nigh
To cautious Sedley's watchful eye,
Who peering through the uncertain light,
Beheld again the visored knight;
But Lenard's signet ring displayed
Gained him free passage to the glade,
Where soon, within the rocky hold,
He sat and heard the story told.
The captain of that dangerous crew
Related briefly all he knew;
How his two men had met defeat,
And made, unscarred, a base retreat:
Wild passion blazed within his eyes,
As, fierce, he cursed the enterprize;—
" For mark," he cried, " Those much I doubt
Who on this mission were sent out;
Methinks the knaves are bought and paid,
Some minions of the law to aid
In capturing of my troops so true,
And all my hard-earned treasures too.

E 3

Doubtless our password has been sold,
And every secret fully told;
But, by the mass, should aught appear,
That is in shape of foeman here,
Prepared at every point we stand,
To meet the traitors hand to hand;
And yon two wretches surely die
Ere light again is in the sky!
Think you, sir knight, the tale is aught
But one from deepest falsehood wrought?
No, by the saints, two, bold and strong,
Had never fled from stripling young.
The challenge too, I well define,
Is but a part of their design;
The cowards deemed that Hugh would fly
At once to seek this vaunting boy,
And thus had I been captive made
By parties strong in ambush laid;
Believing then our caverns grey,
Robbed of their chief, were easy prey:
But when Hugh Lenard's end they boast,
More lives than one shall pay the cost."
"Compose thyself," exclaimed the knight,
"Nor let thy wrath too soon alight
On those deputed to obtain
The maid I fondly hoped to gain;
For if 'twere Rosco's gallant youth,
With whom they had to cope, in sooth,
They had, if loud report be true,
A foe not easy to subdue,
Robust in limb, expert and tall,

Of more than common strength withal.
To me well-known the Roscoes are:
The elder, famed in fields of war,
Has doubless taught his son to fight
As may become a trusty knight;
And if (as thou hast ere now said)
He has his name to thee conveyed,
It has escaped his lips when he
Has spoken out unguardedly;
For long they've held a neighbouring hall,
And deemed their names unknown to all;
But I the truth contrived to glean
From one who had their vassal been,
And who oft told how well the boy
The trusty axe or sword could ply.
Myself to search him out will go,
For, faith, he is a worthy foe;
But though I much admire his skill,
Should he dare claim the lady still,
I'll put his prowess to the test,
And prove the valour of his breast."
Thus as he spoke he rose again,
And hurried quickly from the glen.
Hugh Lenard sat amazed to find
He had not left the gold behind,
And, starting up, he deeply swore,—
" Should he not send the yellow ore,
I'll dog him aye through flood and fire,
To frustrate his most fond desire;
By night and day, through storm and shine,
I'll toil to baffle his design;

Yes, by the saints, revenge most strong
I'll wreak on him that does me wrong."
Thus leave we Hugh, where dark cliffs hung,
With disappointment keenly stung.

Aurora peeped through eastern cloud,
Ere Lockwell reached his mansion proud,
Who straight dispatched an artful spy,
To keep a strictly watchful eye,
Upon the cottage which contained
The gem he late had counted gained;
And bade him mark with faithful care
Whatever might be passing there,
And charged him duly to return
With any tidings he should learn ;
Then, on a downy couch reclined,
Himself to slumber he resigned :
Absorbed in graceless dreams he lay,
Till round him danced the noontide ray.
Meantime the object of his thought,
The being he most wished and sought,
Escorted from the cot had been
Through many a wild and sylvan scene,
The old man serving as her guide;
While Rosco proudly kept her side,
And often wished, as journeying on,
His lot had been a brighter one,
Or that the lady's fortunes were
No more than that 'twas his to share.
Thus while he weighed their separate fates,

They reaehed and paused at Lumbley's gates;
But ere they breathed the word " farewell,"
Thus Rosco strove his love to tell:
" O, sweetest maid, my captive heart
Regrets with thy dear self to part;
Thine eyes have lit a tender flame,
I would but scarcely dare to name ;
A flame which ne'er can die away,
Till every sense in death decay;
A flame which nothing can efface,
Nor distance, time, nor change of place,
But which, with every passing hour,
Shall burn with an increasing power.
To-morrow's sun will see me stride
My noble steed of gallant pride,
Which soon shall bear me hence to where
The heroes of our land repair ;
And, in the midst of sword and fire,
I'll die, or worthy rank acquire,
And aught will dare that mortal may,
Thy smiles to have some future day :
Thy name shall be my leading star,
Through all the thundering shock of war;
And, should I meet a soldier's death,
That name shall be my latest breath ;
Whate'er my fate, where'er I be,
My soul shall still be aye with thee.
Say, empress of my heart, when I
Am far away from that sweet eye,
Wilt thou one fond remembrance own
Of him who lives for thee alone ?"

Here paused the youth, as if afraid ⎫
That in his warmth too much he'd said ; ⎬
But no response the lady made ; ⎭
When thus he did his speech resume :
" Sweetest, if I too far presume,
If, prompted by ecstatic bliss,
My lips have spoken aught amiss,
With bended knee thy humble slave
Shall at thy feet forgiveness crave ;
Let not my words thy anger move,
But pity my too fervent love."
The maid was mute, but he could trace
Approving look in her sweet face,
And her bright eye more stories told
Than lips and tongue could e'er unfold ;
And taking from her bosom fair
A silken braid of her soft hair,
Together with a packet, she
To Rosco gave it modestly ;
Then, with a smile so sweet to view,
She turned and breathed a fond adieu.
In haste he broke the packet's seal,
To find whate'er it might reveal ;
And O, he was a joyful man,
For thus its grateful tenor ran :
" Brave youth, and generous as thou'rt brave,
Whose arm was raised the weak to save,
Think not that Moran's daughter may
Forget thee when thou'rt far away ;
Thy noble bearing might, I ween,
Claim praise of Europe's proudest Queen.

Go seek, as thou hast late designed,
That fame thou well deserv'st to find ;
Go, and upon the battle field
May honour sit upon thy shield ;
May proud distinction crown thy aim,
As great as ever knight may claim.
And know, that Lucia's prayers shall be
Not seldom offered up for thee;
Full oft her arm, in fancy's flight,
Shall guard thee in the sanguine fight;
And, on thy glad return, believe
Her welcome smiles wilt thou receive ;
Then Moran's Lord, who loves the bold,
His child's deliverer shall behold :
Till then, farewell, and may the dart
Of foeman never reach thy heart ;
O may—when thou art hotly pressed—
The God of battles guard thy breast !
Adieu, adieu, rememember me,
For Lucia's thoughts are all with thee."

Young Rosco's heart with rapture leaped,
As lightly on the way he stepped
Towards home, and many a time he sighed
Her name with all a lover's pride ;
Nor dreamed he then, how treacherous foe
Might all his brightest hopes o'erthrow.
But Lockwell's vile and lurking spy
Lay close in secret ambush nigh ;
And all the parting speech had heard,
And saw the silken braid transferred :

Then straight returned he, every word
Reporting to his recreant lord,
Who foamed with boundless rage to hear
That Lucia held young Rosco dear.
Fresh plots of guilt were now devised
And thus the wretch soliloquized :—
" This cursed, this detested boy
Seems formed my wishes to destroy;
But, by the saints, I'll straight prepare,
And follow him to scenes of war,
And there, his visioned hopes to thwart,
Strike this sharp dagger to his heart.
Yes, die he must, and from his death,
My hopes shall draw reviving breath.
O, how 'twill glad my eye to see
His life blood ebbing rapidly !
Then shall I from the battle-plain
Return, and woo the maid again ;
Fresh honours, wealth and fame shall lie
Before the haughty damsel's eye,
And my broad lands of great extent
Will soon ensure her sire's consent.
No mortal knows my late design
To make perforce the lady mine,
Except Hugh Lenard, who will ne'er
Betray the truth to other ear ;
From him no soul may hope to learn
A deed which might himself concern.
Thus far I'm safe, and Rosco's end
I trust not to the dearest friend ;
Myself will do the deed, and I

Alone must see my rival die :
Then, with affected grief, I come
Straight back to Lady Lucia's home,
And feign to mourn, with many a tear,
A friend whom I had held so dear ;
Tell how, amid war's raging tide,
We rode and battled side by side ;
And how he fell with many a wound,
To die upon the blood-stained ground ;
Professing I am charged to bear
His dying wish to Lucia's ear,
The tone of which shall much incline
Her heart to favour my design ;
And thus herself and her rich lands
Will safely fall into my hands ;
And none shall e'en suspect, meantime,
That Lockwell's bride was bought with crime.
Thus, thus, proud girl, thou soon shalt know
One stroke shall all your views undo ;
With trusty sword and lance and shield,
I will betake me to the field,
And doubtless, 'mongst the warriors there,
I shall descry old Rosco's heir,
Whom I must make at once my friend,
Till time shall fitting moment lend ;
Then one bold effort lays him low,
When least he may suspect the blow."
Thus mused the knight on deeds of blood,
Till evening covered field and flood ;
When that soft couch again he prest,
Once more to woo the sleeper's rest.

END OF CANTO FOURTH.

CANTO FIFTH.

Young Rosco rose with morn's first light,
His heart was gay, his hopes were bright;
And Lucia's priceless lock of hair
Around his neck was slung with care;
He donned his mail with warrior's pride,
And buckled broad sword to his side;
Soon, all equipped, on charger true,
He bade his noble sire adieu.
Long time elapsed, and Lucia ne'er
Could aught of her fond lover hear;
But he meantime, 'neath prosp'rous stars,
Was winning honour in the wars;
At Bradoc Down he much obtained,
When Granville's troops the vict'ry gained;
And left he that ensanguined field,
With broken lance and bruised shield.

Its leaves to earth the Autumn cast,
The dreary chilling winter passed,
And yet no tidings came to tell
If Rosco lived, or if he fell.
When cheering spring again came round,
He was amongst the foremost found:
At Stratton, on that bloody hill,
Our hero gathered laurels still;
At Round Way Down he fought and bled,
When Wilmot won, and Waller fled;

There Rosco onward, onward pressed,
And many a knight his strength confessed;
His valour and unerring blows
Struck terror to the boldest foes;
And, step by step, he quickly came
To proud distinction and to fame,
Which gained him many a friendly hand,
Amongst the warriors of our land.
'Twas then Sir Lockwell did appear,
And feigned a friendship all sincere,
But marked, in truth, with jealous eye
His rival's rising destiny;
And oft the noble youth he saw,
From 'neath his corslet gently draw
That braid of hair, that token bright,
Whereon he'd gaze with fond delight;
Which added fuel to the flame,
That urged the wretch to deeds of shame.

Thus time with ceaseless wings sped on,
Till thrice three months had o'er them flown;
And Rosco's bearing pleased the sight
Of England's king, who dubbed him knight;
And through the means of his true sword,
His aged father was restored
To those broad lands he'd been expelled,
And rank and titles proudly held.
Then many a dame of high degree
Looked on our knight admiringly,
And many a maid of noble mien
Would fain, in truth, his choice have been.

But he, sincere as he was brave,
His every thought to Lucia gave;
And oft he longed with haste to fly
Unto the object of his joy;
But daily, hourly broils, that raged,
Still kept him constantly engaged.

At length the royal army sped
To Newbury, with hasty tread,
Resolved to offer battle there
To Essex and his veterans rare,
Who boldly had relief conveyed
To Massey then at Gloster laid;
And thence returning now was he,
With choicest bands of chivalry,
And London-ward their way was bent,
Ne'er dreaming of the king's intent;
But soon brave Essex' piercing eye
Saw royal standards floating high,
And straight with prompt and martial care
His men for battle did prepare.

Anon loud tumult sounding near
Fell on the hapless monarch's ear;
Ten thousand voices seemed to rise,
Reverberating through the skies;
'Twas Essex' troops that came along,
With heavy march and swelling song.
As some the mighty anthem sang,
The brazen trumpets shrilly rang;
The drums boomed deeply on the air,

And banners fluttered proudly there ;
A thousand plumes—oft sullied—waved,
Which had a thousand conflicts braved ;
A thousand spears were glittering bright,
Shewing a grand but awful sight ;
A thousand clanging coats of mail
Strange music flung upon the gale ;
A thousand steeds pranced on the way,
And snorting seemed to chide delay ;
Long trains of guns on rattling wheels
Came slowly rumbling at their heels ;
And onward, like a mighty flood,
They came to deeds of death and blood.
The royal forces saw their foes,
And quick commands amongst them rose ;
Their drums and bugles rang alarms,
And every soldier sprang to arms ;
And two brave armies stood opposed,
Of kith and kindred all composed,
Prepared with weapons dire and dread
Each other's dearest blood to shed :
And as they each the other eyed,
" Advance !" rang out on either side.
That instant phalanx, column, square,
Moved on with swords and sabres bare ;
Next moment, louder than before,
'' Charge ! on them !" echoed through each corps.
With loaded guns and bayonets set,
The foemen in the onslaught met,
And hand to hand, and man to man,
The deadly havoc now began ;

F

Lance struck with lance of warrior true,
Whose bending shafts in splinters flew,
And axes, dealing many a wound,
Brought dauntless heroes to the ground.
With counters barbed each fiery steed
Flew to the charge with lightning speed,
And bore each rider bold and strong
The fierce conflicting storm among :
Like angry waves in narrow bay
They swelled and raged in that affray ;
And flags, which oft in war had flown,
Were shivered there and trampled down,
With corslets bruised, and housings marred,
And morions cracked, and foreheads scarred :
All, all were rushing, crushing on,
Friends, kindred, brothers, sire and son.
The cannon deeply roared the while,
And balls were thinning rank and file,
And carbines cracked and armour rang
Through that dread field with horrid clang ;
And all—where silence late had been—
Became one dark uproarious scene,
A direful scene of bloody strife,
A scene with every terror rife ;
While oft above the deafening noise,
Their leaders' voices still would rise:
" Fire ! Forward ! Charge ! on, on ! ye brave,
To vict'ry or a glorious grave !"
The trumpets ever louder brayed,
As greater carnage there was made,
Their notes commingling with the cries

Of anguish echoed to the skies ;
And infantry and horse were found
Disputing every inch of ground :
The groans of dying men arose,
The parting sobs of friends and foes.
Now this side would advantage gain,
Now that impel them back again ;
And o'er the wounded and the dead
They galloped on with heavy tread ;
While fire and smoke, where sharp blades gleamed,
A murky pandemonium seemed.
Death prowled around with horrid glare,
And reaped an awful harvest there :
That fatal day, in life's full pride,
The brave, the generous Falkland died :
A fiercer contest ne'er was waged,
Nor doughtier men in fight engaged.
And there was not a braver one
Than aged Rosco's noble son,
Who turned his charger left and right,
As though he sought the hottest fight,
Still rushing in through sword and flame,
Urged on by love and thoughts of fame.
His arm was strong and staunch his heart,
His blows fell quick as lightning's dart,
And all opposing, man or horse,
Went headlong down beneath his force,
And naught could hinder his career—
Of death he'd neither heed nor fear—
And oft amid the broil he'd cry,
" Our King, Saint George, and Victory !"

F 2

Then on he sped, while helms were cleft,
And gallant hearts of life bereft ;
And many a powerful charger pressed
Upon the steel that pierced his breast.
Yet still the leaders' cries were heard,
As here and there they hotly spurred ;
" Fight on, fight on, your weapons ply,
And conquer now or bravely die."
Such words seemed newly to inspire
The desperate troops with rising ire ;
But even at the close of day
Stood undecided that affray.
Then as the sun his beams withdrew,
The firing slack and slacker grew ;
The clash of swords began to cease,
And die away by slow degrees,
While martial music's stirring swell
Each moment faint and fainter fell ;
And evening gathered glooming o'er
That dreadful field of death and gore.
Then silence reigned, save here and there
A groan of anguish reached the ear,
Or clank of armour bruised and soiled,
As to the camps the troops defiled.

'Twas then a smile of fiendish joy
Lurked deeply in Sir Lockwell's eye,
Who still by Rosco's side was found,
When thickening clouds were closing round,
Whose shadows suited his dark mind
And that fell deed he had designed.

His victim, ne'er suspecting aught,
Rode on, his breast with pleasure fraught;
His heart, on fancy's rapid wing,
Was far off fondly wandering;
First through the valley, fair and green,
Where Lucia he had heard and seen;
From thence to Lumbley hall he hied,
Where parting words were warmly sighed;
O! what sweet smiles again she gave,
To welcome back our hero brave.

While this bright dream absorbed his mind,
Sir Lockwell hung half pace behind;
No other ear, no other eye,
No other living soul was nigh;
For in the battle's mighty sway
Some distance they were borne away,
Thus causing them alone to ride,
Like many a straggling knight beside.
A glance around Sir Lockwell threw,
Then forth the fatal dagger drew,
And glittered that most treacherous blade
An instant in the darkling shade;
Next moment it was deeply dyed
With crimson streams from Rosco's side,
Who trembling fell from his proud steed,
And sighed " Base murd'rer, why this deed?
Vile coward, may disgrace and shame
For ever rest upon thy name!
O Lucia, all life's joys are o'er,

Bless thee"—the knight could say no more ;
His head fell back, his eyes grew dim,
Convulsive quivered every limb ;
A long deep groan, a death-like one,
Told Lockwell that the deed was done,
Who straight did from his steed alight,
And open tore the corslet bright,
And from beneath took that dear lock,
Preserved through many a battle's shock.
Remounting then he onward sped,
By many a heap of ghastly dead ;
Ere long he reached the camps again,
And feigned to mourn o'er Rosco slain ;
While many a warrior dropped a tear,
Of our young hero's death to hear.
And now the weary soldiers sought
Soft sleep, which many a vision brought ;
Some in their fancies fondly flew
To homes they long had wished to view,
Beheld their wives sweet welcome smile,
And kissed their children oft the while :
Some dreamed of parents old and poor,
And thought they pressed their hands once more ;
While some, on blood their visions ran,
As struggling in the battle's van :
Thus did the mighty hosts repose,
The dearest friends, the direst foes.
Meantime a silence sad and drear
Prevailed, save when upon the ear
The slow and measured footsteps fell

Of stately, watchful sentinel.
But Lockwell, 'mid those slumbering bands,
With guilty heart and blood-stained hands,
Lay waking on his pillow long,
And mused o'er his return to Tong,
Resolving thither straight to fly
With message of base forgery,
Which, to accelerate his scheme,
Should dying words of Rosco seem,
And which, with that soft braid of hair,
He would to gentle Lucia bear.
Thus was his night in scheming spent,
Till morn peeped through the canvass tent;
When royal troops, refreshed, again
Appeared upon the fearful plain,
Prepared the battle to renew,
To perish or the foe subdue.
But Essex, doubtful of the day,
With prudence marched his force away:
Thus thousands fell, and died unshriven,
Yet no decisive blow was given.

The season now was far advanced,
No longer sun beams warmly glanced;
The fallen leaves, the breezes cold,
A fast departing Autumn told,
Which closed, or rather checked awhile,
Intestine broil in England's isle.
The armies weary, worn and spent,
Both into winter quarters went;

And many a gallant youth was free
His friends and kin again to see;
And Lockwell rode with utmost speed,
To crown with falsehood his foul deed.

END OF CANTO FIFTH.

CANTO SIXTH.

And now the clash of arms was o'er;
Terrific cannons ceased to roar;
When homeward to his anxious dame
Full many a wounded soldier came,
While many a lady's heart did mourn
For those who never should return;
And eyes were strained, each passing hour,
From palace, hall, and lofty tower;
And tender hopes, so lately bright,
Were smitten with the general blight.
The dearest ties were torn apart,
With many a love-born broken heart;
Sad widows and their orphans wept,
Of husbands and of fathers 'reft;
And many a once contented home
Became a scene of grief and gloom.

Thus o'er the land intestine broil
Spread desolation, death, and spoil.

The lord of Moran's wide domain,
While far away on distant plain,
Had been by faithful friend apprised
Of plots against his child devised,
And wondered much what wretch would dare
Thus to insult his daughter fair.
Then hastened he with utmost speed
To guard her, should there still be need,
And spurred along o'er numerous miles,
Till, welcomed with her kindest smiles,
He caught her in his longing arms,
And gazed with joy upon her charms ;
Yet saw in her expressive eye,
A mark of deep anxiety ;
And much he feared and shrewdly thought
Her heart with misplaced love was fraught ;
Then questioned her in accents mild :
" Say, dearly loved and only child,
Who dared, in yonder vale, molest
The peace and quiet of thy breast ?
Much would I give the wretch to find,
Be he a prince, a lord or hind."
" I know not,"—was the maid's reply,
" Nor e'en suspicious guess have I ;
But this I know, the youth that came,
And foiled the ruffians in their aim,
Bore valiant Rosco's noble name."
" So much I've heard," the Earl rejoined,

" And thy deliverer yet shall find,
That Moran's Lord can well requite
A deed becoming bravest knight;
But let not, Lucia, thy young heart
Encourage hopes which time may thwart;
Remember, Rosco long exiled
Is not a match for Moran's child;
A worthier baron must, indeed,
My daughter to the altar lead.
Come now, thy sire is sorely worn
And here will rest him till the morn;
Then we together may repair,
Forthwith, in peace our home to share."
Thus said and left the maid,—once more
To doff the weighty mail he wore.

As words which fatal sentence bear
Unto the trembling prisoner's ear,
Were Moran's words to Lucia's heart,
Such anguish did those words impart;
Her gentle bosom heaved and fell
With feelings too acute to tell.
She sank upon a cushioned seat,
Her breast with deepest wo replete,
Such grief, as none, indeed, may prove,
But those of disappointed love:
She owned her father's rightful sway,
And fain would his commands obey;
But rooted in her artless breast,
Were passions ne'er to be suppressed,—
Affections fixed that nought could change,

Nor from her constant soul estrange;
Affections settled deep and true,
Which nought on earth could e'er subdue;
A passion sacred and divine;
And, Rosco, all that love was thine.
What rapturous scenes of blissful days
Her visioned hopes had served to raise!
What joy, what happiness supreme
Was cherished in her every dream!
Her father's words like mildew fell
Upon the hopes she could not quell.
Retiring to her room, she sought
To drown in sleep each painful thought:
But sorrow, with its tears and sighs,
Drove slumber from the fair one's eyes;
And such a night crept slowly o'er,
As Lucia never knew before;
Who, when the morn's refulgent eye
In grandeur decked the eastern sky,
Prepared to leave her kinsman's dome,
And find her own paternal home,
Which reared its turrets, proud and strong,
Not distant far from peaceful Tong.
A week elapsed, a week of fears,
Of care and seldom ceasing tears:
She knew her sire's determined mind
Was ill to bend, when once inclined
To aught that he might have designed;
She knew right well, for oft she'd proved,
How much by him she was beloved;
But likewise knew, though great their state,

His love of hoarding wealth was great;
And sorely feared, for lucre, she
A helpless sacrifice might be.
Yet as the plunging, drowning wretch
At each slight object strives to catch,
So did her pure and artless breast
A thousand slender hopes suggest.
She knew her lover, bold and young,
Was daring as his arm was strong,
And thought, amid the battle's din,
He yet might wealth and honour win,
And never dreamed that treacherous blade
The youth on bloody plain had laid ;
But daily did her bosom yearn,
And looked she still for his return.
One morn, with such reflections fraught,
The lofty balcony she sought;
From thence her long unwearying gaze
Was stretched and strained a thousand ways,
When lo ! far in the distance she
A mounted cavalier could see,
Who forward dashed in utmost speed,
With waving plumes and foaming steed;
And, as he pressed the charger on,
His bright arms glittered in the sun.
O, how she bent her longing eye
The rider's features to descry !
And onward, onward came he still,
And galloped bravely up the hill ;
The rattling hoofs, the armour's clang,
Upon the sylvan silence rang :

He turned to Moran's mansion proud,
Reined in his steed and knocked aloud.
With burning hope her heart beat high,
For now she thought her Rosco nigh,
And deemed he'd come, with wealth and fame,
Her plighted hand at once to claim ;
So much absorbed was her young mind,
In dreams of bliss she ne'er might find.
And sped she to her room away,
To deck her in her best array ;
As though she deemed, in sooth, that he
—The knight—could none but Rosco be.
But scarce arranged was her attire,
When message, from her noble sire,
Requested she would straight attend
On him, and on their warrior friend.
With feelings of much joy the maid
Her father's wish at once obeyed ;—
But O, the tide of anguish swelled,
And her late cherished hopes dispelled ;
For there her disappointed sight
Met not her love but Lockwell's knight,
Whose face a sad expression bore,
And well feigned marks of sorrow wore.
His voice assumed its mildest tone,
As thus he made his errand known :
"Lady, I grieve that 'tis my fate
Such fatal tidings to relate :
O! would some other tongue had brought
The news with so much sadness fraught ;
For deeply I lament to tell
The lot of him I loved so well.

No nobler knight, no braver foe,
Might mortal ever wish to know ;
(I'll mourn his loss with many a tear,
A hero bold, a friend most dear !
For Rosco and myself were bound
In ties of friendship most profound ;
Together on the battle field,
We did our trusty axes wield.)
Alas ! I little thought to be
The bearer of such news to thee."

The lady's colour went and came,
And strong emotions shook her frame ;
A fearful tremour seized her heart,
The blood ran chill through every part.
" O, say the worst," exclaimed the fair,
" Thy words a dreadful import bear ;
O, speak, Sir knight, the worst declare."
The knight proceeds :—" Most lovely maid,
Know'st thou this soft, this silken braid ?—
Rosco, from yonder valiant bands
Returns this treasure to thy hands ;
For he, thou ne'er shalt see again,
Lies dead amongst th' ensanguined slain :
" Dead !"—shrieked the maid in wild alarms,
And sank into her father's arms ;
A pallor o'er her features spread,
Her limbs were helpless, cold as lead ;
A dampness stood upon her brow,
And all unconscious was she now.
Her parent much alarmed to see
His child in death-like lethargy,

In haste her women summoned there,
To tend her with the greatest care.
The knight prepared to take his leave,
Affecting o'er the scene to grieve;
But ere he from the mansion went,
He gave its lord a document,
And said:—" This, couched 'mid flame and swords,
Holds gallant Rosco's dying words;
And swore I, ere he joined the dead,
To bear it unto Moran's maid."
This done, again his steed he strode,
Thus deeply musing on the road:—
" Now, when this sudden flood of grief
Has lent her bosom some relief,
Again shall I assail her breast
With all that language can suggest;
And those few words, that seem the breath
Of Rosco sinking into death,
Will greatly aid my cause, I deem,
And raise me much in her esteem.
Thus far my dearest hopes succeed"—
He thought—and onward spurred his steed.
Meanwhile the lord of Moran's eye
Glanced o'er the packet rapidly;
Its words were few, but every one
Appeared with Lockwell's views to run:—

THE FORGERY.

" Dear maid, my life's blood ebbeth fast,
And all earth's transient hopes are past;

The foeman's steel has pierced my breast,
And soon this form must lie at rest.
But, ere I reach the yawning grave,
One promise of thee would I crave:
Shouldst thou e'er deign thy hand to join
In wedlock sacred and divine,
O, may thy choice on Lockwell fall;
For he is brave and kind withal,
And much has done to aid my aim
Upon the dangerous path of fame.
Unchanging friends we long have been,
Through all war's wild and bloody scene;
And now he swears, on bended knee,
To bear my dying words to thee.
Much would thy faithful Rosco say,
But pain—O Heaven! my senses stray,
A dimness gathers o'er my eyes—
Ah, Lockwell, spare, O spare these sighs!
Farewell! ah me—so soon to end—
O, loving sire—Conyard—my friend—
I faint, I sink, there—let me lie—
Heaven!—Lucia—God—I die, I die."

When Moran had these words perused,
Awhile he o'er their import mused,
And inly hoped his daughter might
Accept of Lockwell's wealthy knight.
And when her mind, as he presumed,
Had somewhat of its calm resumed,
The letter was before her spread,
Which she in writhing anguish read.

Each crafty word, like venomed dart,
Fell on her lone and stricken heart;
She ran it o'er and o'er again,
With every mark of inward pain.

Time rolled along its days and weeks,
And tears no longer stained her cheeks;
But still a secret sorrow pressed
Within her pure and gentle breast:
She'd muse at times the live-long day,
Sometimes would hum a mournful lay;
At times she'd to the balcony,
And eastward stretch her anxious eye,
As if expecting to discern
Her lover yet on his return:
Alas! she still but looked in vain,
And grieving sought her room again.
Meantime the knight his suit had plied,
And at her feet his passions sighed;
In softest terms he vainly strove
To win the constant maiden's love.
Six dreary months had slowly passed,
When Moran thus his child addressed:
"Dearest, thou once could'st cheer thy sire,
With happy smiles or tuneful lyre;
But now alas! he grieves to say, ⎫
Thou never wil'st the hours away ⎬
With artless tale or roundelay. ⎭
Come, cast that sorrow from thy brow,
Which nothing can avail thee now;
Resume thy wonted gaieties,

G

And let bright pleasure light thine eyes :
Vain were thy tears, though seas were shed ;
They never can recal the dead.
Therefore thy griefs at once forego :
A worthy suitor comes to woo ;
The knight of Lockwell's wealthy halls
Is now within our ancient walls,
Who comes to make, with store of land,
The final offer of his hand,
And waits decided answer now :—
Nay, frown not, for, my daughter, thou
Must not despise a suit so fair,
Where thou may'st wealth and honour share ;
The proudest maid in England bred
Might with this knight be fain to wed.
Remember, Lucia, age has now
Its signet set upon my brow ;
Hence we may soon expect that I
Shall with our brave forefathers lie.
Moreover all my hope thou art,
My only child, my dearest part :
From thee must rightful heirs descend,
Our state, our honours to defend ;
And gladly I'd my daughter see
With one united worthily ;
And better is not in the land
Than he who daily seeks thy hand :
Much has he won on battle plains,
With titles proud and wide domains ;
Besides thy Rosco, ere he died,
Wished thee the noble Lockwell's bride.

If, therefore, in thy gentle breast
Thou dost regard his last request,
Or, if thou wouldst a joy impart
Unto thy aged father's heart,
No more the proffered hand reject
Of him who'd love thee and protect.
Refuse me this, and at thy word
Dies every hope of Moran's lord."

" Father," the trembling girl replied,
" Thy will has ever been my guide;
'T has been my pleasure day by day,
Thy every dictate to obey:
Alas! but now appoints that will
A duty painful to fulfil;
For never can I Lockwell love,
Though ne'er so kind his heart should prove.
I own his rank and titled birth,
I praise, esteem, his martial worth;
But think not this can e'er undo
My fervent love for Rosco,—no!
My thoughts to him must ever fly,
Unchanging as yon orb on high.
Deem not that grandeur, gold or fame,
Can ever Lucia's joy reclaim;
Not all the wealth, from shore to shore,
My wonted spirits can restore.
Albeit, my lord, thy daughter still
Would prove obedient to thy will,
She'd sooner pierce her woful breast,
Than see thine own with grief oppressed;

No more I'd wish to tread life's stage,
Except to soothe my father's age:
And though with Rosco bold and brave,
My heart lies in the silent grave;
Yet, should my father will it so,
Indeed my hand I must bestow.
But let this Lockwell still beware,
He ne'er can my affections share;
I ne'er can love again," she sighed,
And pausing cast a tear aside.
" 'Tis well",—the joyful father said,
" Thou still art Moran's duteous maid;
Now do I love thee more and more;
Declining hopes thou dost restore.
Once bound in matrimonial ties,
Thy soul will know fresh rising joys;
Thy husband's kindness soon, I deem,
Will merit Lucia's best esteem;
His tender speech and love shall wean
Thy thoughts from sorrow's cankering vein:
Vain grief, long cherished, shall decay,
As silent time rolls fast away;
Thine eye its lustre shall regain,
Thy voice its soft and cheerful strain;
Thy step its lightness shall resume,
Thy glowing cheek its wonted bloom;
And many a dame of high estate
Shall envy Lucia's happy fate.
Prepare, sweet child, prepare straightway
The richest robes, the best array,
And nine days hence the gallant knight

Shall make thee his by holy rite :
Great joy your nuptial day to crown,
Our gates shall straight be open thrown
Alike to all; the rich and poor
Shall make our halls resound once more ;
The festive dance, the rustic song
Shall wing the cheerful hours along,
And every heart shall be right gay
On gentle Lucia's wedding day."

Thus saying, Moran turned away,
And left his trembling child a prey
To all the torturing pains that rise
From dying hopes and blighted joys.
Her lovely cheek was pale as death,
And short and feverish came her breath ;
Her eye, now robbed of its bright rays,
Was upward turned with steadfast gaze ;
Her hands were clasped, so small, so fair,
In all the anguish of despair.
Thus standing, not a word she spake,
But sobbed as though her heart would break ;
For though she had obeyed her sire,
In this his late and fond desire,
Yet rather would the maid have died
Than thus be Lockwell's plighted bride.
Too well the noble lady knew
Her heart could ne'er be held by two ;
And, with a truly generous mind,
Such as 'twere ever well to find,
She thought her hand, in truth, would prove

A worthless gift without her love;
And wished she might be in the tomb,
Before the wedding morn should come.
Ah, never could she know delight,
If made the wife of Lockwell's knight;
And day by day more sad she grew,
As nearer still the nuptials drew.

Meantime the news of that event
To kindred and to friends were sent;
The tidings, with increasing sound,
Spread through the country miles around;
And e'en to Lenard's cave it flew
Who swore the match he would undo.
At once he planned a sure disguise
To hide him from Sir Lockwell's eyes,
Resolved the promised feast to share,
And to the church attend the pair.
Eight little days soon o'er them went,
In bustling preparations spent;
Another rose, all bright and gay,
The ninth, the joyful wedding day;
Joyful to all, save that young maid
Upon whose mind distraction preyed.
The gates of Moran open flew,
Ere Sol had swept the sparkling dew;
The lark's loud matins rang on high,
Whose melodies enriched the sky;
A thousand birds in brake and thorn
Did usher in the happy morn;
The peasantry, from far and near,

Approached to join the marriage cheer ;
And many a rude musician came
A part in that gay scene to claim :
The old, the young, the weak, the strong,
Commingled in the joyful throng ;
The court was filled—a busy crowd—
And mirth and laughter echoed loud.
Amongst the numbers gathered there,
Sat one whose brow was marked with care ;
An aged harper seemed the guest,
An utter stranger to the rest ;
And though the morning sun was warm,
A long dark cloak enwrapped his form,
Which round his neck was closely laced,
And girdled tightly at the waist.
A cap of minstrel form he wore,
Which one pale bending feather bore ;
The harp was on his shoulder slung,
O'er which his snow-white tresses hung ;
But though the stranger seemed so old,
His dark eye still in lustre rolled ;
His woworn looks such grief expressed,
As won respect from every guest.
Anon, from off his shoulders, he
Took his light harp to join the glee ;
While merry jests went round and round,
Where nought but gaiety was found :
The rural dance, the uncouth song,
Amidst them sounded loud and long ;
From hand to hand the wine cup went,
Inspiring frequent merriment.

Thus did the jocund moments fly,
Until the nuptial hour drew nigh;
And soon the plighted pair came forth,
With friends and kin of rank and birth;
The peasant maidens ran before,
With choicest flowers a plenteous store,
Which on the path were duly spread
That Lockwell and the maid should tread;
Their sweetest notes the rustics played,
The aged stranger lent his aid:
Thus passed the cavalcade along
Toward the ancient church of Tong.
Soon did they gain that hallowed pile,
And slowly marched adown the aisle;
There did the reverend pastor wait,
The nuptial rites to celebrate;
And crowds, of young and old comprised,
Pressed in to see them solemnized.
The parties near the altar stood;
The bridegroom seemed in happy mood;
The maid though rich and rarely clad,
Was all dejection, pale and sad,
And seemed, 'mid that assemblage fair,
Scarce conscious of her presence there.

At length the priest, that holy man,
Slowly the solemn scene began:
" Should any know just cause"—he said—
" Why these should not as one be made,
Let him, e'en now, within this place,
Declare, or ever hold his peace."

A pause ensued, a breath scarce stirred,
And no objecting voice was heard;
But, ere he could again proceed
In gravest tones the rites to read,
A deep stentorian voice did swell,
And on each ear thus calmly fell:—
" I, reverend father, acts long hid
Will shew, this union to forbid."—
" How? where?" exclaimed the wondering knight;
" Who dares impede this sacred rite?"
" I," cried the white-haired harper—" I"—
Confronting him with his reply;
While Lucia stood in deep surprise,
And hope again illumed her eyes;
As looked she on that aged man,
Her blood with freshening vigour ran.
All present now were much amazed,
And on the stranger mutely gazed:
The knight was stung with conscious fear,
But never deemed Hugh Lenard near,
And thought his darkest crime unknown
To all but to himself alone;
And, as a desperate hand he placed
Upon the blade he had disgraced,
He cried again, " Speak, idiot! say,
Who dares my nuptials thus delay;
Proclaim (or from this place depart)
Whence thou hast come, and who thou art."
" Soon shalt thou know," the other cried,
And laid his harp and cloak aside,
Discovering arms and corslet bright,

With belt and badge of trusty knight;
The snow-white locks but false ones proved,
Which were with hasty hand removed,
And dark luxuriant tresses brown
Fell o'er his temples softly down;
And that old man, late stooped and pale,
Was gallant Rosco, stout and hale.
The lady shrieked and swooned away;
Sir Lockwell glared in wild dismay,
And looked on Rosco, pale and dumb,
As on a spectre from the tomb.
Lord Moran gazed perplexedly,
Much wondering what the end might be;
He saw in Lockwell's blenching eye
Strong marks of some deep secret lie,
And now concluded that his soul
Was stained with some dark deed and foul :
The peasants nearer pressed, I ween,
To watch the progress of the scene.
Meantime, Sir Lockwell utterance caught,
And, with fierce desperation fraught,
He snatched the rapier from his side,
And rushing forward, hoarsely cried,
" Fiend ! devil ! if thou still hast breath,
My sword shall yet ensure thy death."
But ere he could let fall his brand,
Another arm had stayed his hand ;
And looking round, he saw, dismayed,
Hugh Lenard there with naked blade,
Who laughed, and cried, with spiteful leer,
" Had this young hero not been here,

To rob thee of thy fancied bride,
Myself with all my care had tried.
Remember, sir, the promised gold
Was never yet to Lenard told ;
And swore I, night and day, to toil
Thy fondly cherished hopes to foil."
Nor stood brave Rosco unprepared
The vengeance of his foe to ward ;
And, when the now unhappy knight
Perceived his wholly hopeless plight,
He rushed away with soul subdued,
By wondering eyes alone pursued.
The robber captain told the tale
Of his engagements in the vale ;
Then stole away, unknown to all,
Long gloating over Lockwell's fall.
But gallant Rosco, word by word,
Explained the rest to Moran's Lord ;
How Lockwell's hand, in friendship veiled,
Had stabbed him on the battle field,
And rifled from his neck the braid,
And left him then and deemed him dead ;
But how by one he had been found,
Who sheltered him and healed the wound ;
Yet how so deep had sunk the blade,
That he had long been helpless laid,
And little hope was entertained
That ever health might he regained :
Still, when he was restored at length
To somewhat of his wonted strength,
He'd ridden down, in haste, to find

If still he lived in Lucia's mind ;
But, ere he reached delightful Tong,
His heart had been most sorely stung,
To know that Lockwell was to wed
His own much loved and loving maid :
How he resolved, in minstrel's guise,
To take the traitor by surprise,
And blast, e'en at the sacred shrine,
The fabric of his dark design.
The maiden, now to life restored,
Gazed on the face so much adored ;
And his dark beaming eyes expressed
The fervour of his faithful breast.
Lord Moran saw their glances fly,
And knew they were of love and joy ;
And, acting a kind father's part,
He blessed them both with all his heart.
The base Sir Lockwell homeward sped,
And soon across the billows fled,
To hide his shame, to hide his crime,
All secret in a distant clime.

A few bright days of bliss were spent,
In undisturbed and sweet content ;
When Rosco to the altar led
The maid who long had deemed him dead ;
And Moran saw with unfeigned pride,
His child a truly happy bride.

END OF THE FORBIDDEN UNION.

A POET'S JOYS.

They may say that the poet's existence is drear,
That his doom is a painful and sorry one here:
They may say, that he spendeth a wearisome life,
In the coldness of penury, terror and strife :—
Go, tell them they err, and they never can know
What rapture at times in his bosom may glow ;
Go, tell them the poet is happier far
Than greatest of statesmen, or chieftains of war.

Give him but the violet with sweet laughing eyes,
The bloom of the branches, the warmth of the skies,
The linnet's soft carol, the throstle's loud song,
Huge rocks in their majesty, founts gushing strong ;
The waving of woodlands, the music of rills,
The flocks in the valleys, the heather-clad hills ;
With these the lone poet is happier far
Than greatest of statesmen, or chieftains of war.

He is ne'er at a loss, how his mind to amuse ;
He has pictures to gaze on, and works to peruse ;
Kind nature supplies him with greatest of books,
In plenty he finds them wherever he looks ;
In the simplest of buds, in the slenderest spray,
In the darkness of night, in the splendour of day ;
O, such yield him joy that no mortal can mar,
Unknown to the statesman, or chieftain of war.

He has pictures in landscapes, and books in the trees,
Finds joy in the sunbeams, and love in the breeze :
The stout spreading oak can a pleasure impart,
A pleasure the purest to gladden his heart ;
In its groan there is worship, and prayer in its nod,
As it bendeth its head to the glory of God :
O, such make the poet, aye, happier far
Than greatest of statesmen, or chieftains of war.

He has joy in the stars as they glisten on high ;
He has bliss in the glance of his child's laughing eye ;
He has joy in the love and the smile of his wife,
Whose kindness can soften the path of his life ;
He has friends who are staunch, he has foes—but no matter--
The former he loveth, nor heedeth the latter :
Then say not he's wretched, but happier far
Than greatest of statesmen, or chieftains of war.

WINTER.

Cold winter hath spread his white sheets o'er the earth ;
All nature seems laid in destruction and dearth,
The clouds hanging heavy, and gloomy and grey,
The sun striving vainly to yield us a ray :
The frost has impeded the roll of each rill,
The sky-lark no longer is heard o'er the hill ;
Not a shrub may be seen, not a leaf on the tree ;
Chilly winter, cold winter, hath few charms for me.

The wretched come shivering, and knock at my door,
And sigh, as they tremble, " Pray pity the poor."
I give them my mite with a heart full of grief,
My mite, which indeed is but scanty relief.
Methinks, were I wealthy, I'd learn to be great
By striving to soften my fellow man's fate ;
For thousands roam forth truly woful to see ;
O winter, cold winter hath few charms for me.

Desolation seems cast over mountain and vale,
No cheerful expression is brought on the gale ;
The plaint of the robin, so doleful and drear,
With lone, pensive cadence falls sad on the ear ;
No soft bud is opening, no floweret is seen,
No butterfly spreading its wings o'er the green ;
No ant is found toiling, no fast-speeding bee ;
O, winter, cold winter hath few charms for me.

Ye wanderers unsheltered, unclothed and unfed,
My heart bleeds to hear you imploring for bread ;
Such things declare something is wrong in the plan,
Since nature yields plenty for each son of man.
How keen must the blast on such beings descend,
Who ramble forsaken by kindred and friend !
Such things at this time rob my heart of its glee ;
O, winter, cold winter hath few charms for me.

Give me the soft violet, the daisy, the rose,
The king-cup, the blossom on hawthorn that grows ;
The beautiful meadows, the clear purple sky,
The thrush in the hedges, the sky-lark on high.

Though sometimes the tempest may pleasure my soul,
When lightnings are flashing, when thunders may roll;
Yet snow-covered landscapes are dolesome to see;
O, dreary, dark winter hath few charms for me.

EVENING WALK.

SPRING.

Beautiful valley, fair Nature's finger
  Once more is painting each meadow and thorn;
Bright Sol is setting, yet his beams linger
  As they were loath to desert thee till morn.
Tender young flowerets are modestly peeping,
  Spring doth its magical influence shed;
All the fair things that in earth have been sleeping
  Rise up again as it were from the dead.

Beautiful valley, fair Nature arrays thee
  Once more in robes I have longed to behold;
Truly, thou can'st from despondency raise me,
  When all thy glories begin to unfold.
O, at the even 'tis bliss to be strolling
  Slow in thy woodlands of sweetest perfume,
When the broad sun to the westward is rolling,
  Leaving thee wrapped in a soul-stirring gloom.

Beautiful valley, where I oft wander,
  Courting the muse in her sylvan attire;
Where softest rivulets twine and meander,
  Teaching fresh notes to my unpolished lyre.
And there is health, there is invigoration
  Wafted on zephyrs that sigh in the shades;
O, there is love, there is pure inspiration
  Found in the depths of thy lowliest glades!

Beautiful valley, the sky-lark is singing
  High in the welkin his evening lays;
Songs of the throstle are merrily ringing,
  Yielding his Maker thanksgiving and praise.
Gone is the winter whose coldness had bound thee,
  Aloft is the wild dove once more upon wing;
Thousands of buds on the trees that surround me,
  Burst into life at the impulse of Spring.

Beautiful valley, how broad are thy meadows,
  Clear are thy brooklets that murmuring flow,
Even like mirrors reflecting the shadows
  Of the huge trees on their margins that grow.
O, I am happy thy dingles exploring,
  Treading such carpets as mortal ne'er made;
While the gay pheasant above me is soaring,
  Proud of the plumage he loveth to spread.

Bards of the North may delight in their mountains,
  Tell of their rocks and their deep roaring streams;
Sing of the crystal that falls from their fountains,
  Sparkling like silver in day's golden beams.

H

Our own native poet may warble as cheerly
    Of scenes where the Aire is rolling along :
I envy them nothing while thou art still near me,
    Beautiful, beautiful valley of Tong.

SONNET.

TO MY MUCH ESTEEMED FRIEND, DR. FIELD.

A loftier harp than mine, dear Field, should raise
Applauding tribute to thy noble heart,
Whose genuine worth full often does impart
A freshening impulse to the poet's lays :
Thy goodness stretcheth far beyond all praise ;
Oft hast thou crushed the thorns before me spread,
And smoothed the path it was my fate to tread.
Whene'er thou saw'st misfortune's thickening maze
Around me gathering, thou wert ready still
To step between, dispelling every ill
That might have cast its influence round my head,
And care, and sorrow at thy presence fled :
Thy lasting friendship yields a thousand rays,
To cheer the poet's soul, and light his gloomiest days.

SONNET.

TO POESY.

Sweet Poesy, soft soother of my dullest hours,
My soul's fair cheerer on life's thorny way!
I hear Thee in each little warbler's lay;
I see Thee in the mighty rock that towers
Above the woods, so gloomily and grey;
I feel Thy presence in the scented bowers;
I meet Thee in the gently passing breeze,
Behold Thee in the waving of the trees;
And Thou dost smile in all the dewy flowers,
In every insect that my glad eye sees:
I find Thee in the storm, the genial showers,
And in the twinkling of the gentle star
That glitters sweetly in its orb afar;
And even in the heavy cloud that lowers
To hide the moon's pale beams, and blot her silvery car.

EXTEMPORE.

TO THE ROSE.

How fair is the rose in its bloom,
That spreads to the genial ray!
But soon all its sweets and perfume
Shall wither and fall to decay.

H 2

An emblem of man is this flower,
  To both the same Maker gave birth :
They flourish, as 'twere, for an hour,
  Then death sweeps them off from the earth.

IT IS NOT THY BROW.

It is not thy brow,
  Though so lofty and fair ;
It is not the flow
  Of thy beautiful hair ;
It is not the blush
  Of thy soft glowing cheeks,
Where crimson hues flush
  When the flatterer speaks:
It is not thine eye
  So witchingly bright,
Like stars of the sky
  So dear to the sight
Of the mariner, lost
  To his friends and his home,
When his vessel is tost
  Amid tempest and gloom:
It is not thy lip,
  Though sweetest of sweet ;
It is not the sip
  Thereon that I meet ;

It is not thy form,
  Though lovely thou art;
No, no, the best charm,
  Dear maid, is thine heart.
Thy innocence, fair one,
  Hath won me alone;
Thy gentleness, dear one,
  Hath made me thine own.

THE OLD HOLLY TREE.

The following lines were occasioned on seeing the remains of an extraordinarily
  large Holly Tree, in the Park Wood, Tong, which was killed by some
  ill-disposed person peeling off the bark.

Alas! it hath perished, and scarcely a bough
Bears remnant of green to acknowledge it now;
Its vigour is blighted, the relic now seen
Is merely the shadow of what it hath been.
How late in its beauty and brightness it stood,
The delight of its Lord, the pride of the wood;
Not an oak, not a pine, waving proudly and free,
Could eclipse the fair robes of the Old Holly Tree.

But now it is silently fading away,
Its leaves falling withered in rapid decay;
Some wretch, of all feeling and tenderness void,
Its death blow hath given, its nurture destroyed;
And now towards earth it is drooping its head,
As though it were seeking the home of the dead.
O, wo! to the hand, whose soe'er it may be,
That has stolen the life of the Old Holly Tree.

Long, long it has flourished in health and in bloom,
Unchanging its freshness, in sunshine or gloom;
Whatever wild hurricane over it came,
Its grim spreading branches were still found the same.
No more shall the red berry hang from its arms,
Grim Death has come o'er it and stricken its charms;
Its aspect is mournfully dreary, and we
Lament the sad fate of the Old Holly Tree.

Like all that is mortal, it had but its strength
A moment, as 'twere, to be plundered at length;
Like all that is mortal, mild, tender, or stern,
From earth it arose, and to earth shall return;
And the sprays that could gladden the visitor's eye,
In their parent's cold bosom forgotten shall lie;
No more shall the breeze shake its foliage so free,
For nought can restore us the Old Holly Tree.

Now the redbreast is singing a dirge o'er its death,
Who perhaps 'neath its shadows received his first breath;

The linnet is silent* who once gave his lays,
And builded his home 'mid the holly's thick maze,
Where he cheered his soft mate with a full swelling breast,
As she brooded with care in her little round nest;
Where he taught his young offspring to whistle in glee,
And to pour forth their praise to the Old Holly Tree.

For a hundred of summers it held up its form,
And smiled through the winters at tempest or storm;
Yet, though it could conquer the heat and the blast,
Man, cruel destroyer, could blight it at last.
He may boast of his intellect, greatness and worth,
But he's still more destructive than aught upon earth;
He devotes to his purposes all he may see,
From the rush to the oak, or the Old Holly Tree.

The strong winds are sighing with deep mournful swell,
As though they were breathing a parting farewell;
The towering oaks droop their heads by its side,
As though they were wailing the loss of its pride;
Ye'd think, as the stream murmurs near, that it said,
" Ah me, the brave Holly is withered, and dead!"
Yet still the remains have attractions for me,
The wasting remains of the fine Holly Tree.

[O, yes

---

* It was winter when I saw the blighted tree, which accounts for the
linnet's being mute.

O, yes we may read, in its aspect so grave,
A thousand stern precepts for monarch or slave;
There's a language in each of its leaves as they fall,
There is wonderful eloquence found in them all;
There's a voice that can tell us all, truly and plain,
That life's little pleasures are transient and vain;
That the princes of earth, howsoe'er great they be,
Shall crumble and fade like the Old Holly Tree.

The stoutest, the weakest, the little, the great,
Are all, smitten Holly, approaching thy fate;
The fairest, the bravest, the noblest, the mean,
Appear, and glide quickly from life's narrow scene;
Earth swallows her thousands as time passes o'er,
And death, ever ready, supplies her with more;
Not a thing shall escape, but perish like thee,
Thou once blooming beauty, thou noble old tree!

LIFE.

A FRAGMENT.

Life! what is life? 'tis like the curling smoke
Ascending from the embers into air;
We see it rise, but turn again and look,
'Tis vanished, faded, gone, we know not where:
'Tis like soft flowers, or trembling leaves of green,
On waving branches, smiling fresh and gay,

This morn in all their natural beauties seen,
To-morrow dashed by stormy winds away :
'Tis like that hour a tender maid may love,
When stolen from a parent's watchful eye,
To meet though jealous guardians disapprove,
The youth on whom depends her future joy ;
O, what an hour of bright ecstatic bliss,
What floods of rapture swell each lover's heart!
But ah, they scarce have pressed the burning kiss,
Ere they again, reluctantly, do part ;
The bell proclaims the stolen hour is gone,
While they, o'erjoyed, believe it but begun.

Thus, thus frail life, when hungry Death appears,
How short, how little seem a hundred years !
Man, poor weak being, on the bed of death
Seeks to retain the quick departing breath ;
Years idly spent are pictured to his eyes,
And thoughts on thoughts of bygone days arise !
His school-boy scenes, long, long since passed away,
Are as a dream, a dream of yesterday ;
With pain he thinks on all his wasted time,
Of youthful vigour, manhood's health and prime,
When vain ambition led his heart and eye,
And wealth, and power, and pride were all his joy ;
Ne'er thinking death so wondrous soon might come
To fit him for his last estate, the tomb :
And now he sighs, 'mid fast increasing pain,
" O, would that I could spend this life again,
Improved I'd live ;" but ah, he sees too late ;
Death flings the dart and seals his earthly fate.

ON SEEING THE SEXTON ENTER THE
GRAVE-YARD, TONG.

Again to his toil is the old man repairing,
Whose footsteps are feeble, and silvered his head;
With mattock and spade he'll be shortly preparing
Another cold cell for the home of the dead.
Ah! fellow mortal, disturb not my dear one,
She who my loneliest moments beguiled;
Touch not the green sod that covers my fair one,
Stir not the grave of my beautiful child.

For 'twas a flow'ret I proudly did cherish,
With love the most fervent, the fondest of care,
Hoping to see its maturity flourish
Sweetly in tenderness, bloomingly fair,—
But the destroyer crept into its blossom,
Its little heart piercing as softly it smiled:
O, aged sexton, afflict not my bosom,
By marring the grave of my beautiful child.

She was a treasure I deemed all perfection,
The love of my soul, the delight of mine eye,
Nourished in deepest, in warmest affection,
Affection that but with my being can die.
White-headed mortal, thy implements waken
A storm in my bosom, a tumult so wild;
Ne'er let the verdure that springeth be taken
Away from the grave of my beautiful child.

She was all gentle and innocent-hearted,
Replete with bright purity, sweetness and worth ;
Dearest of angels, too soon we were parted ;
Thou, thou wert too good for the rude scenes of earth.
O little daisy, that springs in March bleakness,
Thy modest eye opening calmly and mild,
Dear spreading emblem of infantine meekness,
Bloom on the grave of my beautiful child.

Then, then will I kiss thee as thou art unclosing
Thy charms o'er the ashes that crumble beneath,
I'll fancy the dew on thy petals reposing
Are tear-drops thou fondly hast shed o'er her death.
The rude winds of winter were sullenly sweeping
In gusts round the Church that shall ne'er be defiled ;
The tall trees above bowed down, as if weeping
With me o'er the fate of my beautiful child.

Ah can I forget when, in gay summer hours,
I sat with my babe in the thorn's cooling shade ;
When her little soft fingers could scarce pluck the flowers
Arising in gentleness round where she played ?
But while such sweet emblems about us were spreading,
And all in their innocence blushingly smiled,
I never once dreamt that, as those might be fading,
A grave might be made for my beautiful child.

'Twas even so then, and my soul was left lonely,
Robbed of a gem which made my heart light;
Had Death stolen all but my little one only,
Her presence had made life's gloomy way bright.

Still must we submit to the will of High Heaven ;
'Tis sinful to grieve over hopes thus exiled :
Yet we cannot but mourn when the death-blow is given,
To one so beloved as my beautiful child.

O, white-headed sexton, tread lightly above her ;
O, mar not the sod in the lone place that grows ;
Touch not the willow that waves gently over
The cold silent spot where her relics repose :—
What homes for the dead have thy hands here provided,
What numbers on numbers thy labours have piled ;
But ne'er to thy care was a sweeter confided
Than she, my own loved one, my beautiful child !

ACROSTIC.

F ast speeds this life of care and woes ;
A like with all, on, on it goes,
R unning like a rapid stream,
E ven like a short-lived dream.
W hat is Death? a pilot drear,
E ver ready, always near;
L onesome guide ! by Him are we
L ed on to dark Eternity.

TO JANE.

While on mountains lambs do play,
While the sunbeams bless the day,
While the skylarks sing in May,
     Dearest Jane, I'll love thee!

While the earth produces corn,
While the dewdrops deck the thorn,
While the thrush proclaims the morn,
     Dearest Jane, I'll love thee!

While the little busy bee
Hums in spring from tree to tree,
While the fishes swim the sea,
     Dearest Jane, I'll love thee!

While in summer daisies grow,
While in winter falleth snow,
While the brooks and streamlets flow,
     Dearest Jane, I'll love thee!

While the moon bestows her light
On the darksome shades of night,
While the stars do shine so bright,
     Dearest Jane, I'll love thee!

While the eagle high doth soar,
While the rolling billows roar,
Till I'm cold, and am no more,
     Dearest Jane, I'll love thee!

EVENING HOURS.

Sweet evening hours ! calm, silent and serene,
Fair fitting time for contemplation this,
When lightest zephyrs mildly, kindly kiss
Rosebud and woodbine on each hedgerow green ;
When twilight hangeth o'er this much loved scene,
Like the deep shadow of a sombre pall ;
While soft refreshing dew-drops gently fall,
Moistening the soil where scorching heat hath been;
When happy birds have ceased their noisy mirth,
And a bright star peeps through heaven's azure screen,
Lending its halo to this lovely earth :
A thousand flowerets close their modest eyes,
Soon as the sunbeams leave the gay green sod;
And solemn thoughts within my heart arise
Of Nature's wondrous works, and of creation's God.

Sweet evening hours ! ye truly can repay
The toilsome duties 'tis my lot to fill :
Thus wandering forth by many a brake and rill,
My mind forgets the turmoil of the day,
And heartfelt pleasures light me on my way,
Through the deep vale, so lovely and so still,
Breathing pure odours of the new mown hay :
Or sauntering onward through the woody shade,
Where oft the poacher's midnight snare is laid,
And by the brook, and up the oak-clad hill,
Where many a time my wayward feet have strayed ;

While deep reflections through my bosom steal,
And reverential awe of Heaven's correcting rod;
All things above, below, around reveal
The changeless love, the power, the presence of a God.

Sweet evening hours ! still lovelier ye appear,
As thicker shades are gathering slowly round ;
And all seems now in slumber wrapped profound,
As though death reigned in awful grandeur here,
So placid all, so solemn, and so drear.
The peaceful village, place I love the best,
Lies undisturbed in sweet, in tranquil rest ;
The old Church stilly nestles as it were,
Beneath the trees which o'er its hallowed form
Their green arms spread, a shield from heat or storm,
Whose foliage flings a deeper, darker gloom
O'er the lone yard, and over many a tomb
Of those departed, those our hearts held dear ;
Of those who doubtless, when in health and bloom,
Where now I tread full many a time have trod,
And truly felt, and owned the presence of a God.

CHRISTOPHER KEMPLAY, PRINTER, LEEDS.

CPSIA information can be obtained at www.ICGtesting.com
Printed in the USA
BVOW021102101011

273260BV00009B/27/P

9 781165 143320